The
**Princeton
Review**

Writing Smart

Junior

The Art and Craft of Writing

by C. L. Brantley

Random House, Inc. New York
www.randomhouse.com

To Klaatu and his friend Gort

ISBN 0-375-76261-2

Second Edition

Manufactured in the United States of America.
10 9 8 7 6 5 4 3 2 1

CONTENTS

Introduction

THIS BOOK WAS MADE FOR YOU

The last thing you need is another textbook or a ton of extra quizzes to do, right? We agree with you—textbooks are boring and quizzes are a pain. So don't worry. This book is different. *This* book is an adventure. It is the story of three kids named Bridget, Babette, and Barnaby, and a huge, gruff cat named Beauregard, and their perilous Quest for the Lost Art of Writing. Their quest takes them to many strange lands where they meet a colorful assortment of weird characters who help them find the information they need to complete their quest.

Be warned: Should you choose to follow them, you might wind up learning some pretty valuable writing skills—stuff like how to write good letters, how to do research reports for school, how to write magazine articles, and how to create poetry and stories. That's not our fault, though. We have no intention of teaching you anything. Whatever skills you pick up from this adventure story are purely accidental, and . . .

Okay, okay. You caught us. Yes, *Writing Smart Junior* is designed to teach you writing techniques. The title kind of gives it away, doesn't it? But what makes this book different from your other workbooks and textbooks is that the whole time we were creating it, *you* were all we thought about. What would someone like you find appealing? What would it take to keep someone like you interested in learning about writing? What are some of the things you hate—or like—about writing?

We did our best to make a book you would enjoy and refer to often. There are a few quizzes, but they are only there so you can check your progress. There are also some exercises so you can practice your skills. The exercises aren't things you need to sit down and do like homework, though. They are meant to help you get your "writing juices" flowing, so do them at your leisure.

By the way, we weren't kidding about the adventure story. It's in here, alright, complete with river rafting, parachuting, lions, flamingos, deserts, safaris, big fat carp, and bottomless pits. You'll see.

How to Use This Book

This book is part handbook and part odyssey. To use it as a handbook, whip it out whenever you have some kind of writing project you want guidance on. Use the table of contents to find the section you need. For example, if you need information on doing library research, you'd turn to chapter 4, Welcome to Fort Report. Or, if you can't remember the proper format for a business letter, you would turn to chapter 3, The Better Letter Inn.

Now for the odyssey part. An odyssey is a long, adventurous journey. As we said before, this book includes an adventure story, but that's not what we mean. Learning to write well *is* an adventure in itself. The more you write, the more you learn about yourself, others, and life in general. What better odyssey is there? We hope *Writing Smart Junior* is your first step in a lifetime of fantastic writing adventures.

Chapter 1

Dine and Dash at the Mute Café

I should say right off the bat that I do not—repeat, do not—consider myself some kind of protector of stray humans. I must admit, younger humans are awfully cute, but I make it a policy to let them make their own mistakes while I happily mind my own business. Regular kids just get into regular trouble, so there's usually no harm done. But I'll tell you, extraordinary kids seem to get into extraordinary trouble, so recently I've had to make some exceptions to my policy. Those exceptions are named Bridget, Barnaby, and Babette.

Bridget seems ordinary at first, just a smart-mouthed American kid with a bad bubble-gum habit. Barnaby is a science genius, but other than that he doesn't seem too weird, except for his crazy, bushy hair. And Babette is a French girl who is just too cool for words. So what's so extraordinary about them? Suffice it to say that I had barely recovered from my last round of adventures with them when I saw them in the park again—and I tell you I could smell trouble brewing. Yessir, just like the smell of a pile of burning tractor tires. When those kids get together, there's always something about to go wrong. So, I figured I'd better keep an eye on them for a little while.

Oh, dear me. I'm always getting ahead of myself. I must introduce myself. My name is Beauregard, a well-bred, gentleman cat from South Carolina. Aside from my remarkably good manners, my most striking features are my elegant, moist nose (or so some have said), my carefully groomed paws, my glistening black fur, and my size—I'm four feet tall when standing upright.

But this story isn't about me. This is the story of how Bridget, Barnaby, and Babette reclaimed the Lost Art of Writing. It wasn't easy, believe me. Here's how it all began.

✎ ✎ ✎ ✎ ✎

Bridget, American by trade and New Yorker by nature, was getting impatient with her parents. What was supposed to be a one-week stay in Paris had been extended to two weeks because her mother said, "You can't really know a city unless you *live* it." Well, as far as Bridget was concerned, the only things Paris had to offer were art museums, statues of naked people, and bad television. Thankfully, she had made a couple of friends who kept her from dying of boredom. At least, most of the time.

"What do you want to do today?" asked Babette, a very mysterious French girl who dressed entirely in black and wore retro sunglasses. Very stylish.

"I don't know," sighed Bridget. She lay back in the soft grass, lazily blowing a huge bubble with her gum, letting it pop, then sucking it noisily back into her mouth. "What do you want to do?"

"Let's not start that again," said Barnaby, their boy-genius friend. "If you can't come up with something to do, I'll just go back to the lab and resume my gym-sock experiment."

"What's stopping you from coming up with ideas?" demanded Bridget. "Does being a science wiz automatically make you a bad social planner?"

"Fine," said Barnaby. "Let's play that card-throwing game you showed us yesterday."

Bridget heaved a sigh but reluctantly agreed. She took off her Yankees baseball cap and laid it bottom-up in the grass about ten feet away from them.

"There. Who's got the deck of cards?" she said.

"Cards. Cards," mused Barnaby, searching his pockets. "I know I had them somewhere. . . ."

Barnaby began scratching his head. But his was no ordinary head. Barnaby had an amazing, wild, huge bush of hair that actually came in very handy sometimes—as in this case, for example, when something suddenly fell out of his hair and onto the grass.

"Let me guess," said Bridget. "A deck of cards?"

"Actually, no," sighed Barnaby, picking up the item. "It's a wad of French money. Small bills. I guess it's not so bad, but to tell you the truth, I'd rather have some cards."

"Nonsense," said Babette, suddenly sitting up and snatching the money out of Barnaby's hand. "Money equals entertainment. Come, we can all go have a hot chocolate or lemonade at a café."

No one had a better idea, so they all got up, brushed the grass off themselves, and meandered toward the street.

But there are many, many cafés in Paris, each with its own special, and sometimes peculiar, atmosphere. Bridget, Babette, and Barnaby were in that kind of bored funk that makes you want very much to do something, yet somehow makes it impossible for you to make any decisions or come to any agreement about what you want to do. One by one, they checked out and passed up every café they came to. "Too crowded," Babette would say.

"Too French," Bridget would say. "Too symmetrical," Barnaby would say. Finally, after too much walking, they found themselves on a street with no name in a neighborhood they didn't recognize. They were very thirsty and just a little irritable.

"I still say we should have gone into that one with the neon hamburger in the window," grumbled Bridget.

"Oh, stop it," snapped Babette.

"Look, I don't care where we go now. I just want to sit down," said Barnaby. "How about that place there? It looks like a café."

The place Barnaby pointed to did look like a café, but there was something strange about it. It was very old and neglected, indeed, a bit sad. It was on a corner of the street, which is generally a good place for a café, but no one was in it. In fact, no one was anywhere. The street was completely empty. Even the other buildings on the street, which also were old and neglected, seemed empty too.

Babette hesitated for a moment but decided she might as well have a cup of hot chocolate. Bridget agreed, and they crossed the street and entered the little restaurant.

The inside of the café looked like something out of another time. The light was dim. The tables and chairs were made of dark wood. The long bar had a dull brass rail. Yellowed, framed posters for operas and plays hung on the cracked walls. Barnaby, Bridget, and Babette quietly made their way to a table in the corner.

They sat silently for a good long while. There were no waiters and no other customers. A burst of sunlight from the doorway finally shocked them out of their inability to speak. An elegant, moist nose appeared, followed by a large, shiny black paw.

"Beauregard!" exclaimed Bridget. "Boy, am I glad to see you."

Beauregard the cat slinked over to the table and offered his head to her for petting, which she supplied with some vigor.

"I'm glad to see the cat too," said Barnaby. "For some reason, I feel a little safer when he's around."

Beauregard, a fine southern aristocat from South Carolina, had accompanied Bridget, Babette, and Barnaby on several adventures and misadventures in the past. He made it his business to keep an eye on them when they needed it, which, unfortunately, had been pretty often recently. He didn't like to seem too concerned though, so he usually just curled up and slept, or appeared to sleep, which is what he proceeded to do under Bridget's legs.

"Hmm," chuckled Babette. "Beauregard is the sleepiest cat I know."

Bridget smiled, but her smile faded when she saw the shadowy outline of a man who was watching them from the other side of the room. She gestured to Barnaby and Babette with a nervous jerk of her head, and they turned slowly around to look.

The man moved soundlessly toward them. As he came closer they could see he had round glasses and a neatly trimmed beard and mustache. He wore a white shirt and black tie and held a large white dishcloth in his hand.

"Um, hello there," said Bridget, trying to act calm. "Two lemonades and a hot chocolate, please."

The man stared at her blankly. Babette tried placing the same order in French but got the same reaction.

"Hello? Can you hear me?" asked Barnaby, snapping his fingers.

The man fixed a cool stare on Barnaby. "I *heard* you. You want two lemonades and a hot chocolate."

He turned and moved silently away, returning a few moments later with their drinks. The thirsty kids drank them with great relish while the mysterious waiter stood and watched.

"And with what do you propose to pay me?" he asked when they had finished.

"We have over twenty francs," said Babette, waving the wad of money at him.

"We do not accept money here," said the waiter.

"You mean you only take credit cards?" asked Bridget.

"No. No credit cards. Only writing—*good* writing."

"I am sorry," said Babette. "We do not have any books to offer you."

"You misunderstand me," said the man. "I don't want a book that has already been written. I want *you* to write something for me. Each of you must contribute since you all had a drink."

Babette and Barnaby looked rather puzzled. Bridget fidgeted uneasily. In the first place, she didn't consider herself much of a writer, and in the second place, this waiter gave her the creeps.

"Yeah, uh, sure," she said, getting up and backing away from the table. "I'll come right back and write you a couple poems, or something. I just need to check something outside. . . ."

As she turned to make a break for the door, a deafening crash of thunder ripped through the air, lightning zapped through the darkened sky, and buckets—no, *tubs*—full of rain began pouring down on the deserted street. Bridget stared sadly through the little window. Behind her, she heard the *swishhhh* of a match being struck, and smelled a sulphury burning smell. She turned to see the waiter lighting the candles on the tables. The room had become rather dark.

"Looks like we're in for a storm," he said. "I think you'll find it will clear up if you take care of your bill, however."

"What kind of café is this, anyway?" cried Bridget, suddenly feeling very trapped.

"This," said the waiter, "is the Mute Café. Mute, as in 'not speaking.' But I want to change that. I want to bring the words back. I want to talk about writing. And *you* are going to sit here and listen."

Bridget walked quietly back to the table and resumed her seat.

Chapter 2

Gearing Up for the Quest

"The Mute Café, huh?" said Bridget. She suddenly felt annoyed with this guy. "That's kind of a funny name for a place where you have to pay with writing."

"I used to call it the Muse Café," said the waiter, ignoring her tone. "Do you know what a muse is?"

Barnaby, Bridget, and Babette shook their heads.

"A muse is an inspiration. It can be a person or place, just someone or something that excites you to create. Musicians have muses. So do painters and dancers. But people don't seem to have any inspiration for writing anymore. No one comes in to talk about their books and their essays. No one even comes in to write letters nowadays. The words are gone." The waiter shook his head sadly as he gazed at the storm raging outside.

"Don't feel bad," said Barnaby. "It's just progress. We don't need writing anymore. Instead of writing letters, you can actually talk to someone on the telephone. Isn't that better? And who needs books when you can watch television?"

"No!" shouted the waiter. "Don't you see? Writing is one of humanity's greatest gifts. Writing is a joy and an art all its own. Written and spoken language is what separates us from dumb animals, like that cat there under the table."

Beauregard opened one eye and growled softly. *He* had certainly written a few tender little love poems in his time. He considered arguing with the man, but the rain made him drowsy, and he went back to sleep. The kids shifted about uneasily.

"You came here for a reason, you three," the waiter continued. "To put the *s* back in *muse*. To bring back the words. To reclaim the Lost Art!"

Babette, Bridget, and Barnaby cringed. This guy was getting really odd. Luckily, he sensed that he was being a little overpowering, and he calmed down a bit.

"I see I'll have to take a more practical approach," he began. "We'll start with what concerns you most—school. In school, you are probably being asked to write reports and papers, right? How do you like it?"

"It's about as much fun as having my teeth drilled," said Bridget. Babette and Barnaby nodded in agreement.

"Well, I say that's because you have no clue what you're doing," he said. "Now, before you get mad, let me explain. I'm not saying you don't know how to read and write and spell. But that's not the same as writing something that other people can read and understand. You may know how to catch and throw and run, but that doesn't necessarily make you a good baseball player."

Bridget perked up at the sudden change of topic and gave the waiter her full attention.

"If you don't know what you're doing, baseball isn't much fun. And unless you're blessed with rare athletic skills, you don't get good at it unless you practice, right? But once you get the hang of it, it's great. Well, it's exactly the same thing with writing. You have to understand the ground rules and master a few basic skills in order to have fun."

Babette, Bridget, and Barnaby were all listening closely, but the man had stopped speaking and was staring back out the window.

"Yes?" said Barnaby. "What's your point?"

The waiter looked at him. "Not to put any pressure on you, but the water is beginning to gather in the streets. I fear the end is near for this café, and that would be a great shame. If you don't bring back the art of writing, it will be lost forever."

"Yeah, but mister, like you said, we don't have the skills," said Bridget. She didn't like the way the guy had sucked her in by talking about baseball before switching back to writing. "Besides, we can't go outside. So just what are we supposed to do?"

"I can give you the supplies you'll need to start out with. Then you can begin your quest in the cellar."

"The cellar. Right. Lots of mysteries down there," Bridget scoffed.

Babette shot her a warning look. She always gave that look when Bridget got rude or sarcastic.

"We would be pleased to help you," said Babette nicely. "Besides, we still owe you for our drinks. If you please, give us whatever supplies are needed to recover the Lost Art that you speak of."

"Thank you. You don't know how important this is—not only for me, but for yourselves too. You'll understand that soon. Now, you probably already know these things, but we should review the basics. Here is a list of terms you should know."

A GLOSSARY OF TERMS

Adjective—A word that describes a noun or pronoun, like the *rotten* banana, or the *itchy* scalp, or the *odd* waiter.

Adverb—A word that modifies a verb or adjective.

That's a *very* ugly dress.

He ran *quickly* to catch the bus.

Agreement—A grammatical term meaning that the *subject* (see below) of a sentence is matched with the proper form of the verb. Singular subjects (only one person, place, thing, or idea) must have singular verbs, and plural subjects (more than one) must have plural verbs. It is very important to identify the subject correctly—don't be distracted by other words and phrases between the subject and verb.

Only one man *goes* moonwalking at a time.

If all three men *go* moonwalking at the same time, there is no one to look after the rocket.

Are Dorothy and Toto going to make it back to Kansas?

Is the Cowardly Lion really cowardly? Neither the Tin Man nor the Scarecrow *is* cowardly.

The meeting of the pipe fitters *was* called to order. (Even though "pipe fitters" is plural, the correct verb is "was," not "were," because the subject of the sentence is "meeting," which is singular.)

Each of the boy scouts *is* responsible for packing his own lunch.

All of the boy scouts *are* wearing clean underwear today.

Note: Agreement is a very tricky part of grammar. There are many rules and special cases to learn, and even the best writers get confused sometimes and have to look up rules in their grammar handbooks. Please use your grammar book or *Grammar Smart Junior* to review subject-verb agreement if you need to.

Analogy—A comparison showing that two things have several things in common even though at first this doesn't seem to be the case.

Learning to write well is like learning to play baseball: You have to understand the ground rules and build up some basic skills before you can have any fun.

Conjunction—Words that link other words and phrases together.

Chew your gum vigorously *and* blow big bubbles.

I like grapes *and* kiwis *but* not figs.

Contraction—A shortened word, or two words shortened and stuck together, usually with an apostrophe to show where letters are missing.

You use them all the time, *don't* you?

Yes *ma'am*, I'll do the dishes.

Salt *'n'* vinegar potato chips are my favorite.

Interjection—This is a word or phrase that doesn't really do much except express feeling, and it's not usually grammatically connected with other parts of speech. Some interjections are: Wow! Phew! Ouch! Zoiks! D'oh!

Metaphor—A comparison that describes one thing as another, usually using the word *is*.

The moon is a big cream pie in the sky.

The muddy road is a red ribbon laced through the green hills.

Noun—A person, place, thing, or idea.

Charles is a terrible *driver*.

The only *foods* he'll eat are *cauliflower, applesauce,* and *beets.*

Proper nouns are specific people and places, like *Los Angeles* or *Samantha*, and they are always capitalized. *Common nouns* are not specific, like *city* or *girl*.

Object—The part of a sentence that receives the action.

Stan kicked *the football.*

Marcia cut *her hair.*

Parallelism—Matching different parts of a sentence structurally and grammatically.

Some of the fun activities at the park include rowing boats, riding bikes, and climbing trees.

Laughter was her gift, sorrow was her curse, and chocolate was her weakness.

If the parts of a sentence that form a series or group don't match correctly, it's called *faulty parallelism*, which is a grammatical error.

Preposition—A word showing the relationship that nouns and pronouns have to each other.

The leeches were *on* Kevin's thighs.

The pumpkin fell *between* the two police officers.

I stuck my hand *into* the mouth *of* the manatee.

Pronoun—These words work just like nouns, but they are noun substitutes.

He rides a camel to work. Why doesn't *he* give *her* a ride on the camel? *I* say the camel belongs to *him*, but *she* says *it* belongs to *them*. *You* are the camel's best friend.

Pronouns can be *possessive*, which means they show belonging. Possessive pronouns include: *my, mine, your, yours, his, her, its, our, ours, their, theirs*. Sometimes these words are considered to be adjectives as well as possessive pronouns.

Simile—A comparison that uses the word *like* or *as*. Similes are less complicated than analogies.

He has a head *like* a cantaloupe.

She's *as* stubborn *as* a grass stain.

Subject—The person or thing that performs the action of the verb in a sentence.

Money is the root of all evil.

The overwhelming tide of letters and presents surprises Grandma every time her birthday rolls around.

Verb—Verbs are action words. They tell what the nouns and pronouns are doing. Sometimes, the nouns and pronouns aren't doing much except "being," but states of being are verbs too.

The soup *is* hot.

Water *cascaded* over the edge of the bathtub.

Uncle Joe's belly *jiggles* when he walks.

✎ ✎ ✎ ✎ ✎

"To make sure you have mastered these basics," said the waiter, "try these quizzes. If you have any trouble, you should review your grammar until you feel comfortable with it."

✍ QUIZ #1 ✍
The Parts of Speech

In the following passage, certain words are **bolded.** Decide what part of speech the bold word is, and then write your answer in the blank next to the word. Write "n" for noun, "pro" for pronoun, "adj" for adjective, "adv" for adverb, "int" for interjection, "v" for verb, "prep" for preposition, and "conj" for conjunction.

The first **thing** _____ that struck Manfred's **eyes** _____ was a group of his **servants** _____ **endeavoring** _____ to raise something that appeared to him a mountain of **sable** _____ plumes. He **gazed** _____, without believing his **sight** _____.

"What are **you** _____ doing?" cried Manfred, **wrathfully** _____. "Where is **my** _____ son?"

A volley of voices replied, "**Oh** _____ ! My lord! The prince! The prince! The **helmet** _____! The helmet!"

Shocked _____ with these **lamentable** _____ sounds, and dreading he knew not what, he advanced **hastily** _____; **but** _____ what a sight for a father's eyes! **He** _____ beheld his child dashed to pieces **and** _____ almost buried **under** _____ an **enormous** _____ helmet, a hundred times more large than any casque ever made for human being, and shaded **with** _____ a proportionable **quantity** _____ of **black** _____ feathers.

from *The Castle of Otranto*, Horace Walpole

✍ QUIZ #2 ✍
Coming to Agreements

In the following sentences, underline the subject, and circle the correct form of the verb given in parentheses.

1. Each of Lorraine's sons (has, have) a frog and several pet otters.

2. Mandy's collection of rubber chickens, clown noses, and brightly colored wigs (were, was) respected throughout the entire circus world.

3. (Is, Are) Kevin and Kyle coming to camp this summer?

4. All of the girls in Smallville (wear, wears) bows in their hair.

5. Mathematics (is, are) my best subject in school.

6. My bride Patricia, my wife and my love, (arrive, arrives) on the steamer from Portugal today.

7. Bees and pollen (irritate, irritates) me the most.

✍ QUIZ #3 ✍
What Kind of Comparison?

In the following examples, mark "A" in the blank if the comparison is an analogy, "M" if it's a metaphor, and "S" if it's a simile.

___ 1. Stefano's eyes were limpid pools of Caribbean water glistening in the sun.

___ 2. Watching Uncle Louie dance was like watching Jell-O on springs.

___ 3. Love is sometimes like an avocado in winter: You have to pay a high price for it, it can be very hard at first, it tends to rot before it ripens, and you find out too late it was mainly a big pit.

___ 4. Larry's feet were like two canoes with leather soles.

___ 5. The sun, her cheeks blushed red with embarassment, hid her face behind the horizon.

✎ ✎ ✎ ✎ ✎

"Got it?" asked the waiter.

"No problem," responded Babette gallantly. "I am ready to begin the quest."

"Not so fast," he replied. "We have something else to review—a little thing called punctuation."

PUNCTUATION

Period . Use a period at the end of a sentence to signal that the sentence is complete. A period is a full stop.

Comma , A comma is used to show a brief pause rather than a full stop. Commas separate things in a series and separate independent thoughts that are connected with *and* or *but*. They also set off introductory phrases from the rest of a sentence.

> For example, I like armadillos, pecans, and papyrus, but I don't like you.

> **Note:** Many people disagree over whether you should use a comma before the final *and* in a series. That is, whether it should be "rabbits, cats and dogs" or "rabbits, cats, and dogs." We are in favor of using the comma before the *and*, but you should do whatever your teacher or your heart demands.

Semicolon ; One of the more misused pieces of punctuation, the semicolon is like a long comma or a short period. It signals a break or pause between thoughts, but not a full stop.

> Myra's new haircut was a disaster; she refused to take her hat off for weeks.

> It was impossible to get Melvin and the Melometers to play at the party; instead, we hired Zoltag the polka master.

Sometimes semicolons are used to separate things in long, complicated lists.

Canada offers skiing, hiking, and moose-goosing; Aruba has snorkeling, blowfishing, and tippling; and Kansas City gives you roping, branding, and barbecuing.

Colon : Use a colon before a list of items, after a formal greeting in a letter, or as an introduction to a long quotation or statement.

Patriot Patrick Henry is famous for one line: "Give me liberty or give me death!"

You'll need several things before exploring the bear cave: rope, a flashlight, canned peas, and a good pair of running shoes.

Question mark ? You know how to use this, right? Question marks are used at the end of sentences that are questions. Do you understand?

Exclamation mark ! Use these at the end of sentences to show strong emotion or emphasis. If you use them too often, they lose their strength, so use them sparingly, like hot sauce.

I hope I make myself understood!

Put that armadillo down right now before it eats your hand!

Dashes — Dashes are often overused and misunderstood. They should be used to show a shift in thought in a sentence or to set off a piece of a sentence dramatically from the rest of the sentence. Dashes are dashing bits of punctuation but, again, they lose their zip if you use them too much. Before using one, ask yourself whether or not a couple of commas would work just as well. Save your dashes for truly exciting tidbits.

Anne Boleyn—a woman with twelve fingers, rumor has it—was executed when her husband King Henry VIII got tired of her.

Please remember to bring me that purple— oh, never mind.

Quotation marks " " Quotation marks go around a sentence that someone has spoken. In stories, they show a character's spoken words. In newspaper articles and papers, they set off the exact words of a person, or information taken word for word from another source, such as a book. Quotation marks are also used around titles of articles, poems, songs, essays, and other short works.

"Will this plague of frogs never end?" whined the pharaoh.

"Hand me that piano," said George.

In his poem "The Bells," Edgar Allan Poe taps his toes "to the tolling of the bells, of the bells, bells, bells, bells, bells, bells, bells."

Parentheses ( ) They set off background information, side thoughts, explanations, and digressions from the rest of a sentence or paragraph. Parentheses can hold short phrases or entire paragraphs, depending on how long your side thought is. If your sentence begins and ends within parentheses, the period is placed inside the final ")". If only part of the sentence is inside the parentheses, the period goes outside.

Note: One "(" is a parenthes*i*s, and two "( )" are parenthes*e*s.

> Mary had been gorging herself on cookies for three weeks (she always had a weakness for sweets) and managed to gain twenty-five pounds.

> (William Faulkner, an American writer, was very fond of using parentheses in his books. Sometimes he goes on and on with some parenthetical side story for so long you forget it's not part of the regular story, then suddenly you see that ending parenthesis, but by then you've forgotten what the regular story is about. That was okay for him, though, because he won the Nobel Prize for Literature.)

Apostrophe ' Apostrophes show possession or missing letters in a contraction.

> I wear children's clothing. Don't you think that's strange? You wouldn't think so if you could see ladies' clothing on me.

> James is my brother. James's socks smell revolting.

Note: When the noun is singular, the apostrophe goes before the *s*, as in *boy's* or *Glenn's*. If the noun is plural but doesn't end in *s*, the apostrophe still goes before the *s*, as in *children's* or *women's*. *But*, if the noun is plural and ends in *s*, as most of them do, the apostrophe goes *after* the *s*, as in *the nuns' habits* or *the strikers' demands.*

Italics *Italics*, or *slanty writing*, is used for the titles of major works like books, movies, newspapers, and magazines. (Remember, quotation marks are used for shorter pieces like articles, essays, and poems.) Italics are also used to emphasize a word or phrase. If you have a computer, you can probably italicize words quite easily. If you don't have a computer or you usually write things out by hand or on a typewriter, you can show that you mean a word to be italicized by <u>underlining it</u>.

> Teddy vacuums, dusts, washes dishes, and does the laundry, but he will *not* empty the cat litter.

> Have you ever read the book *Mrs. Frisby and the Rats of NIMH*?

✎ ✎ ✎ ✎ ✎

"Whew," said Barnaby. "That's quite a long list! Okay, are we ready now?"

"Not just yet," replied the waiter. "We'd better see whether or not you really know what you're doing. Punctuation can be a dangerous thing if not used wisely."

✍ QUIZ #4 ✍
The Perils of Punctuation

Use commas, semicolons, and colons to punctuate the following sentences correctly.

1. When planning my birthday party I decided I wanted cake ice cream and candy instead Mom gave us carrots yogurt and prunes.

2. There are three essentials for enjoyable road trips chocolate doughnuts sunglasses and a good selection of heavy metal cassette tapes.

3. I'm afraid we're all out of the yellow leather miniskirts however I can offer you this polyester parka.

Use dashes to punctuate these sentences correctly.

4. I saw a three-toed sloth considered a delicacy by the natives, who stuff it with pineapple and serve it at feasts slowly make its way down the diving board, where it paused briefly before doing a swan dive into the pool.

5. We used Christmas lights both yellow and white to decorate the gloomy hallway.

6. Get me the hammer the big heavy one in the black toolbox so I can squash this bug.

Use quotation marks and apostrophes to punctuate these sentences, and underline anything that should be in italics.

7. Lets go see the latest Jim Carrey movie, The Drooling Idiot, at the theater tonight! yelled Mark, but Staceys stereo was turned up so loud she didn't hear him.

8. Carol was reading one of her mothers books, Poems About Armadillos, when she ran across a poem called The Pouting Armadillo that was so sad she was moved to tears.

9. Both of my sisters hairstyles are so scary they look like they should be starring in The Bride of Frankenstein.

10. Fido just hasn't been the same since Mr. Johnsons cat took over his doghouse, said Pete.

✏ ✏ ✏ ✏ ✏

"Well?" demanded Bridget, not all that patiently. "That water outside is still rising, so we'd better be on our way."

"Yes, I suppose you'd better," said the waiter. "I can't tell you exactly what it is you'll be looking for, but I will tell you this: There are Five Basic Rules for Good Writing. Discover these Rules, and you will complete the quest and save the café from flooding. And just to get you off on the right foot, I'm going to tell you what the first Rule is."

"Sounds like cheating," Barnaby commented, but the waiter ignored him.

RULE #1
Rules are made to be broken—but only on purpose.

"So the first Rule is that it's okay to break the rules?" asked Bridget. "What's up with that?"

"No," said the waiter. "The Rule says you must break rules only on purpose. That means you have to *know* the Rules before you can break them. That way, you'll know *why* you're breaking them."

Barnaby, Bridget, and Babette looked confused. Their teachers always took points off their grades if they broke the rules of grammar and punctuation. The waiter smiled at them.

"Don't worry," he said. "You'll understand in time. At least I hope you will, for all our sakes. Now, quick, into the cellar, all of you."

Chapter 3
The Better Letter Inn

Well, of course I followed the kids into the cellar. I couldn't very well let them try to save the art of writing on their own, could I? But I must say I regretted my decision almost as soon as the waiter closed the large, heavy door behind us. It was a dark, dank basement, damp and chilly perhaps because of the rain outside. I also heard the scurrying of little feet that did not belong to any of us, which didn't bother me, since I am a cat, but it seemed to spook my companions, who huddled close together as they made their way down the stairs.

Barnaby, Bridget, and Babette stood very still while they tried to let their eyes adjust to the darkness. They didn't have much luck, though. It was so dark even I couldn't see.

✐ ✐ ✐ ✐ ✐

"Hmmm," said Barnaby, scratching his head. "I don't think we can do much searching if we can't see anything."

"I might have picked up some matches from the table," offered Babette, who began searching her pockets.

Suddenly, there was a loud thud.

"Ouch!" yelled Bridget. "Something just fell on my foot."

"Uh, sorry," said Barnaby. "I just knocked something out of my hair. Can you find it?"

Bridget crouched down and carefully began patting around on the ground. "Ugghh," she groaned. "This place smells. Wait! I think I've got it."

She stood up, and the darkness was pierced with white light.

"Bless that hair of yours, Barnaby," said Babette. "A flashlight is just what we needed. Let's look around."

Bridget shined the flashlight around the cellar. At first, they saw only what you might expect to see in the basement of an old Parisian café: stacked-up tables, wine bottles, candlestick holders, wooden casks. Everything seemed to be covered with a thick layer of dust. But then, on a shelf behind them, they saw a stack of very new-looking pencils, pens, folders, and notebooks.

"Well, isn't that convenient?" Bridget commented. "Looks like that waiter laid out some supplies."

Beauregard says before starting any writing project, make sure you have the essentials:

- plenty of paper—it helps if it's in a notebook, so you don't lose any of the sheets

- pencils and pens

- a folder to keep your work in

They each gathered up what they wanted but seemed confused about what to do next. Then Beauregard, sensing that the kids weren't likely to make any sort of decision soon, decided to take matters into his own paws. He walked back up the stairs and began scratching at the cellar door. Barnaby turned around to look at him.

"I think Beauregard has the right idea," he said. "Maybe we should go back out and ask that guy for a clearer explanation of what we're supposed to be doing."

Babette and Bridget readily agreed. They climbed up the stairs to join Beauregard, reached for the door handle, and pushed. Nothing happened. They jiggled the door knob and pushed again. Nothing happened again.

"Uh oh," said Barnaby. "You don't suppose he locked us in?"

"No," said Bridget, shining the light on the doorjamb. "It's not locked. Just stuck."

She began beating on the door with the end of the flashlight and calling out for help, but none came. After a few minutes, she gave up and turned to Babette.

"I know there's not much room, but do you think you could manage one of those amazing karate kicks of yours?" asked Bridget.

"I thought you'd never ask," said Babette. "Step aside, please."

Beauregard, Bridget, and Barnaby moved out of the way to let their friend go to work. She took a few deep breaths and closed her eyes. Then, rearing back, she let out a hair-raising "Hiyah!" and kicked the door with her right leg. A second later, a blinding light shone through the opening, and the kids and the cat fell flat on their faces in what seemed like dirt.

When they stood up, they were not in the Mute Café as expected, and the cellar behind them had vanished. Barnaby, Babette, Bridget, and Beauregard shook themselves off. They appeared to be in the middle of a wide street in what looked like a town from the Old West. Behind them was a weathered, wooden building with a sign painted on it: "The Better Letter Inn." Below the sign was a pair of swinging double doors, and between the doors was a tall, muscular woman in a simple brown dress who stood glaring at them.

"And *stay* out!" she yelled, turning and going back into the inn.

The kids were dumbfounded. Had they just escaped from the cellar or had they just been kicked out of an inn? They stood blinking at each other in confusion. A crackling laugh finally brought them to their senses. As their eyes adjusted to the sunlight, they saw an old man with a scraggly white beard moving to and fro in a rocking chair on the wooden sidewalk beside the doors.

"Heh, heh! Hedda don't like strangers, no sir, but especially not strangers who can't even write a simple letter. Heh, heh, heh!" the old man laughed.

"What's all this?" snapped Bridget. "We just got here. I don't know anything about a letter."

"That's what I'm saying, little miss," chuckled the old timer. "You just dropped in out of nowhere. Hedda wants you to state your business in writing, but you couldn't, so out you went!"

"But why does she want a letter? Isn't talking just as good?" asked Barnaby.

"Well, son, there are lots of reasons letters are important, and lots of reasons people want letters instead of talk," he replied. "Just you take a look at this list."

- **Letters give you a written record.** People like to save letters of requests, actions, directions, promises, and demands so they can refer to them later, usually for business purposes. Such letters become important documents.

- **Letters can be shared.** Sharing your letters with more than one person over time means you don't have to have the same conversation over and over to give one message to many people. In business, letters are often passed around so the right action can be taken or decisions can be made. But be careful—For that same reason, it's not always smart to put private stuff meant for one person in a letter unless you're sure you can trust that person.

- **Letters show what kind of person you are.** Well-written letters show that you are smart and educated. Employers, colleges, and other institutions want to know you can write.

- **Letters are powerful.** Letters can go places and do things you can't. For example, you'd have a hard time putting a phone call through to the president or some other important, busy person. But letters are solid and real. If you're a good, persuasive writer, your letter will be passed along to that important person, who will read it when he or she has time. Good letters get noticed— and acted on.

- **Letters are cheap.** You can write pages and pages to your friends and family and send them for just a few dimes. Talking to people is great, but letters can be saved and read again and again. Besides, getting letters from friends and family is fun.

- **Letters can be thought out.** Sometimes you can say things in a letter that you can't say out loud, because when you write a letter, you can think about exactly what you want to say and how you want to say it. Some special letters are kept and valued for years and years.

❀ ❀ ❀ ❀ ❀

"Wow," said Bridget, chewing her gum thoughtfully. "I never looked at it that way. What exactly does this Hedda lady want from us again? It seems kind of complicated."

❀ ❀ ❀ ❀ ❀

"Well, no, not really," the old timer said, pulling a pipe out of his overalls. "There are really only two basic kinds of letters, **friendly letters** and **business letters.** Not that business letters can't be friendly. It's just a matter of format."

"Can you show us?" asked Babette.

"Why, sure," he said. "By the way, the name's Frizzy."

Babette introduced herself and her friends.

"Pleased to meet you all," said Frizzy, nodding his head politely. "Now, bring me that notebook you have there."

The old man sketched out the format for a friendly letter.

FRIENDLY LETTERS

Date
Salutation,
    Body_____
_____
_____
_____
_____.
    _____
_____
_____
_____
_____.
    _____
_____
_____
_____
_____.

Closing,

Name

Parts of a Friendly Letter

- **Date**—That's obvious. Just write the date, like "March 9, 1888." That way, the reader knows when you wrote the letter.

- **Salutation**—*Salutation* is a fancy way of saying "greeting." Usually, people write "Dear So-and-so," but you don't have to in a friendly letter. If you want to write "Yo, Poodlehead" or "Hey, Sis," that's just fine. The usual punctuation after the salutation is a comma.

- **Body**—Here's where you say whatever it is you have to say. And even though this is a friendly letter, you should watch your grammar and express yourself clearly. Break your thoughts down into paragraphs. Remember, you won't be there to clear up misunderstandings. In conversations, you can use your hands and facial expressions to get your point across. The other person can ask questions. But in a letter, you have one chance to get it right, so think while you write.

- **Closing**—This is what you write before ending the letter. In a friendly letter, people often end with "Love" or "Your friend" or "Yours truly." Other options are "Your loving sister/brother/whatever," "Best regards" or "Sincerely." In a friendly letter, you should write whatever expresses your feelings best. The closing is usually followed by a comma.

- **Name**—Here's where you sign your name. If the person you're writing to isn't a very close friend, write out your first and last name.

Beauregard says friendly letters don't always have to be friendly, and they're not always written to friends and family. Friendly letters are letters written for non-business reasons, usually to people you know. But you don't have to know the person to send a friendly letter. You can write letters to your favorite celebrities, to people you hear about in the news, like people who are sick in hospital, or to anyone else you feel like. Try it!

✎ ✎ ✎ ✎ ✎

"Well, that's seems easy enough," said Bridget.

"Fine, then, let's see you give it a try," said Frizzy, rocking in his chair. "Write a friendly letter to Hedda explaining who you are and how you got here."

Bridget wrinkled up her forehead in thought for a minute, then wrote the letter.

March 9, 1888

Dear Hedda,

My name is Bridget, and my friends Barnaby, Babette, Beauregard, and I are searching for the Lost Art of Writing. To tell you the truth, we're not exactly sure how we got here. A little while ago we were stuck in the cellar of a café in Paris, which is hard to explain, but I'll try.

I am from New York City, and I have been traveling in Europe with my parents. I got to know Babette (she's French), Barnaby (he's a science genius), and Beauregard (the big black cat) in Paris, and we've been through a lot together. Most recently, we went to a café for something to drink, and a strange waiter whose name I don't know told us we had to pay him with good writing. I thought he was crazy and tried to leave, but it started raining really heavily, and he told us we had to figure out the secrets of good writing or the café would be washed away in the flood.

We really didn't have much of a choice. He told us to start in the cellar, so we did. When we tried to leave the cellar, we wound up here. We really meant no offense to you. If there is any way you can help us, we would be most grateful.

Yours truly,

Bridget B.

"Well done, Bridget," said the old-timer. "It's straight to the point and very clear, even though your story is a bit outlandish. I suggest you stick to the truth whenever possible."

"That *is* the truth!" snapped Bridget, stomping her foot.

"Calm down, little miss, I'm not saying it's not the truth," laughed Frizzy. "Like I said, that's a good letter. But we might want to try a more formal approach to Hedda, too, then see which one works better. Hand me that notebook again. I'm going to show you how to write a business letter. And pay attention, because this is kind of complicated. You have to stick to the Rules and write as clearly and directly as possible."

Beauregard says paragraphs are your pals. Whenever you write—not just letters, but any writing—group your thoughts into paragraphs. Paragraphs are groups of sentences that share a topic or deal with the same idea. The first line of a paragraph is usually indented five spaces (or sometimes a line is skipped between paragraphs). There are no hard rules about paragraphs, but here are some guidelines:

- Start a new paragraph whenever you begin a new thought or topic.

- Try not to write an entire page without starting a new paragraph.

- Give important ideas emphasis by giving them their own paragraphs.

Using paragraphs makes your writing easier to understand and more enjoyable to read.

BUSINESS LETTERS

Date
space
space
Name
Title/Department
Company name
Street address   } **Inside address**
City, State ZIP
space
Salutation:
space
   Body _____

_____

_____

_____.

_____

_____

_____.

Closing,
space
space

space
space
Printed name
space
Your initials/typist's initials
Enclosure
cc:

✎ ✎ ✎ ✎ ✎

"Yikes, that's really confusing," groaned Barnaby. "What does it all mean?"

"I'm glad you asked," replied the man, puffing on his pipe. "Here's a rundown."

Parts of a Business Letter

- **Date**—This is the same as in a friendly letter. Write the date, like "June 3, 1996" or "August 21, 1922." *Don't* write "June 3rd" or "August 21st" or "April 2nd." The numbers are clear enough without the *st*, *rd*, or *nd*.

- **Inside address**—The inside address looks just like the address you'd put on the front of an envelope. No one is sure exactly why you have to repeat the address on the letter, since the person receiving the letter knows what her or his own address is, but that's the rule. The parts of the inside address follow.

- **Name**—Write the full, proper name of the person you're sending the letter to, *and be sure you're spelling it right*. People get upset when you don't bother to spell their names correctly. Also, make very sure you use the correct title—Mr., Ms., Mrs., Miss, Dr., or whatever. Unless you are certain that a woman you are writing to prefers Mrs. or Miss, it is usually best to use Ms. before a woman's name.

- **Title/Department**—If you know the title or position the person holds in the company, something like "Vice President of Ditch Digging" or "Executive Coordinator, Stamp Sorting," include it. If you don't know the title, leave it out and include the name of the person's department instead, like "Accounting Department" or "Customer Relations Department."

- **Company name**—This is the full, formal name of the company.

- **Street address**—The number and street of the company. Make sure you include the suite, room, or floor number if you have it.

- **City, State, ZIP**—Exactly what they say.

- **Salutation**—In a business letter, you usually don't address a person by his or her first name. "Dear Mr. Peterson:" or "Dear Ms. Wainright:" would be the correct form of greeting. At some point, you might have to write a letter but won't know the name of the person you are sending it to (this often happens with complaint letters or job applications). In that case, "Dear Sir or Madam:" would be the greeting. Note that in a business letter, the greeting is followed by a colon, not a comma.

- **Body**—Business people are very busy. That's why what they do is called "business." Make sure your letter is brief and to the point. In fact, you should try not to write business letters that are longer than a page unless you really must.

  The first paragraph of the letter should explain why you are writing. If you are asking for some sort of action—like a refund for something you bought or a job interview—say so right up front. The next paragraph or paragraphs should provide background information. Include only the most important information. The final paragraph can briefly restate your purpose for writing, thank the reader for her or his time, and provide a telephone number or address at which you can be reached if necessary.

  Style and tone are important. Be clear and polite, even if you are writing to complain about something.

- **Closing**—It's best not to sign a business letter with "Love." It'll look silly. Instead, use "Sincerely" or "Yours truly." After the closing, which is followed by a comma, skip four line spaces.

- **Signature**—In the area left by the four spaces, sign your name in cursive. Use a blue or black pen. Colored ink or pencil aren't serious enough for a business letter. Don't dot your *i*'s with little hearts or smiley faces, and don't make any curlicues or swirls. Business people rarely have time for humor or decorations, so remember: be serious and dignified.

- **Printed name**—This is your name written or typed out, so the person responding to your letter will know how to spell your name (signatures are sometimes hard to read).

- **Your initials/typist's initials**—You won't have to worry about this for now, but just so you know, at the bottom of some business letters, you might see something like "SBJ/km." The capital initials belong to the person sending the letter, "Samantha B. Jefferson" maybe. The lowercase initials belong to the person who typed the letter, usually the assistant of the person with the big initials—maybe "Kevin Martin."

  If you type or write your own letter, it isn't necessary to put your initials on it. Someday, when you're a big shot and other people type your letters, they can take care of this little detail for you.

- **Enclosure/cc:**—These are two other little details you'll find in business letters. If you are sending something along with your letter, like a brochure or photographs, it is proper to write "Enclosure" at the end of the letter so the person receiving the letter knows something is supposed to go with it. The reason for this is that business people often have other people open their mail for them, and things can get misplaced or left in the envelope.

The letters "cc:" mean that a copy of the letter was sent to someone else. The name of that person (or those people) will appear after the "cc:".

✎ ✎ ✎ ✎ ✎

"I think I have a headache," said Bridget.

"Well, no one ever said writing a business letter was fun," said Frizzy. "But you have to learn to do it properly. You'll probably have to write your fair share of them in your lifetime, so you might as well get good at it. Here, now, why don't you try writing Hedda—her last name's Gabbler. Here's the address."

Bridget groaned but took up her pen and pad and began.

March 9, 1888
Ms. Hedda Gabbler
Owner and Proprietress
The Better Letter Inn
100 Main Street
Writeway, TX 12345

Dear Ms. Gabbler:

My name is Bridget, and my associates, Babette, Barnaby, Beauregard, and I are on a quest for the Lost Art of Writing. We stumbled upon your inn by chance and deeply regret any offense we may have given you. If you can assist us by pointing us in the right direction, we would be very grateful.

As for how we came here, I will be brief: We were having something to drink in a café in Paris. The waiter demanded that we pay him with "good writing." We were unable to do so, and were unable to leave the café because of a heavy rainstorm. The waiter made it clear the rain would flood the café unless we discovered the Lost Art of Writing and paid our bill, and he suggested we begin our search in the cellar. We did as he suggested, but when we tried to leave the cellar, we found ourselves in your inn, not in the café.

Again, we would appreciate anything you could do to help us. Should you wish to contact us, we can be reached out in the street in front of the inn. Thank you for your time and consideration.

Sincerely,

Bridget B.

"Bridget, I really think you have a knack for this," said the old timer after reading her letter.

Bridget smiled and blushed a little, pleased at the compliment.

"Now, then," he said, turning toward Babette and Barnaby. "Which one of these letters do you think will work best with Hedda? You don't know her well, but try to think which one she'd like."

Barnaby and Babette read through Bridget's letters a couple of times and thought a while. After a few minutes, Babette spoke up.

"Ms. Gabbler is a strong businesswoman," she began, "but we are not coming to her for business reasons. I believe she wanted only to know why we were in her inn. I think the friendly letter is best for her."

Barnaby agreed.

Beauregard says neatness counts. If you need to write a business letter, it's best if you print it from a computer or type it on a typewriter. If you don't have access to a typewriter or computer, print your letter neatly (except for your signature, which you write in cursive) in blue or black ink.

"Good," said Frizzy, fumbling in his overall pockets for something. "I think I might have some envelopes here somewhere . . . yep! Here they are. Gather around, y'all, and let me show you how to do this right."

Frizzy laid out two envelopes on the back of the notebook Bridget handed him, flap-side down, so he had a nice smooth writing surface.

Selecting one, he started to write:

ENVELOPES ARE EASY

✎ ✎ ✎ ✎ ✎

```
Your name                                          ┌─────┐
Your street address                                │STAMP│
Your city, your state and ZIP                      │    ¢│
                                                   └─────┘

                 Name
                 (Title/Department—for business letters)
                 (Company name—for business letters)
                 Street adress
                 City, State ZIP
```

✎ ✎ ✎ ✎ ✎

"Easy as pie," said Barnaby, writing out the envelope and handing it to Babette.

She put Bridget's friendly letter inside and sealed it.

"Now what do we do?" she asked.

"Well, I'll be taking that letter to my wife!" said Frizzy, standing up and taking the letter from the wide-eyed Babette. He grinned at them, then turned and walked through the swinging double doors.

"His wife?" whispered Bridget after Frizzy had disappeared into the inn. "I sure am glad I didn't say anything rude in those letters."

The three adventurers waited outside for what seemed like an eternity, staring around at the town and kicking their feet in the dirt. Bridget blew bubbles to amuse herself. Beauregard fell asleep beside Frizzy's rocking chair in a warm patch of sun. Finally, they heard some heavy footsteps from inside, and Hedda burst through the doors and out into the street.

"You poor children!" she exclaimed. "You've got a lot of learning ahead of you. Come inside and eat something."

They were all hungry, including Beauregard, so in they went. Hedda fed them stew and potatoes until they were totally stuffed.

"You aren't lost, you know," Hedda said. "This is just the first stop on your journey.

You've already learned something, you see? You now know how to write letters."

Babette, Bridget, and Barnaby looked at each other in wonder.

"But I can't tell you where to go from here. It's your quest, and you have to go where it leads you," she said. "I will make a suggestion, though. There isn't another town for miles. You might find it easier if you travel by boat. There's a river at the edge of Writeway. You might be able to flag down a passing raft or boat that would take you a ways."

"Thank you," said Babette. "And thank you for the food."

"You'd best be on your way," said Hedda, showing them to the door. "Things are probably getting soggy in Paris."

✍ EXERCISE #1 ✍
Greetings, Spaceboy

Zorkzork is a boy your age from a planet far, far away. He is very interested in having a pen pal on Earth. Write Zorkzork a letter inviting him to come visit some time. Tell him about life in your town—what people do for fun, what your typical day is like, what the climate is like. Remember, he's never been to Earth, so make sure you describe things well.

✍ EXERCISE #2 ✍
Consumer Comments

Think of a product—like your favorite candy bar or soft drink, your sunglasses, your bicycle—that you enjoy a lot. Come up with a few examples of how the product has helped you or a few reasons why you think the product is better than others like it. Write a letter to the president of the company that makes the product and tell him or her what you think.

or

Think of a product that has been a big disappointment to you. Maybe something you bought was broken, didn't work the way it was supposed to, or didn't do what you expected. Come up with specific reasons for your disappointment. Write a letter to the customer service department of the company that makes the product, and tell them what you think.

(If you actually do send these letters, you'll be surprised at the response you get. Most companies take the letters they receive very seriously. Try it!)

Chapter 4

Welcome to Fort Report

I could have stayed and lapped up that beef stew for weeks! Besides, Writeway had made me a little nostalgic. Back in the days of my young cathood, I was friends with a sheriff in a dusty old Texas frontier town—I was his deputy, you might say. I had a beautiful lady cat friend at the time named Miss Whiskers. Ah, sweet Miss Whiskers! I'd come back after days away hunting down criminals, and her soft purring and scratchy tongue behind my ears made me forget all my troubles. If only I hadn't . . . well, what's done is done.

Anyway, Bridget, Barnaby, and Babette headed in the direction Hedda pointed, and soon we reached a fairly decent-sized river. As you might have noticed, Bridget doesn't have much patience, so she decided right away that waiting for a boat to pass was a stupid idea. Barnaby may be a science genius, and Babette may be a karate expert, but

Bridget had a few abilities of her own. That bubble gum of hers, for example, always came in handy.

❧ ❧ ❧ ❧ ❧

"Stand back, you guys, I'm going to make us a boat," said Bridget, standing at edge of the river. Her jaws and cheeks began pumping furiously as she prepared to blow an enormous bubble. But this would not be just any bubble—it would be a bubble boat.

Babette and Barnaby looked at each other with some concern. It wasn't that Bridget didn't blow good boats, just that they always seemed to get in trouble when traveling in one of her bubblecrafts. For instance, Bridget blew great hot-air balloons, but they always got swept off course by the wind or punctured by birds. However, it didn't look like any other boats were coming, so they decided to chance it. When Bridget finished they climbed aboard beside Beauregard and shoved off.

The river flowed along at a comfortable clip—not so slow as to be frustrating and not so fast as to be frightening. As they drifted along, people sometimes waved to them from the banks. They decided not to stop. They were on a quest, after all, and when you're on a quest you have to go with the flow.

They had all gotten pretty relaxed and were enjoying their river ride when Barnaby noticed what looked like a walled-in city in the distance on the left bank. An artificial fork in the river headed directly toward the walls.

"Hey!" cried Barnaby, shaking his friends out of their daydreams. "I think we're being sucked in!"

"What?" asked Bridget, rubbing her eyes and staring in the direction he was pointing. "But, Barnaby, it's only a little canal. We'll probably stay on the main river."

Bridget settled back down into the bubbleboat and closed her eyes.

"Unless I miss my guess, that little canal, as you call it, feeds a hydroelectric dam near the walls of that fort," said Barnaby in his most scientific voice. "The fort probably gets all it's electricity by harnassing the river currents. We most certainly *will* be pulled in that direction by those currents, and we could be hurt!"

Bridget sat back up. Babette was alert. Even Beauregard was awake. And sure enough, the boat was being pulled faster and faster toward the city walls.

"Bridget, I do wish these boats of yours were easier to steer," said Babette, trying not to sound as though she was complaining.

"If only we had something to use as a rudder," she replied.

Barnaby began scratching his bushy head and thinking. Babette nudged Bridget, and they both looked at him hopefully. Suddenly, a Ping-Pong paddle fell out of his hair and into the boat.

"So that's where it was!" cried Barnaby, picking up the paddle.

"Quick, Barnaby," said Bridget, "that paddle just might work. Get in the back of the boat and try to steer us to shore."

But it was too late. The water had pulled them right up to the wall and through a narrow opening. They burst into the fort on a great rush of water, but it became calm almost immediately. Looking around, Bridget noticed a man in a blue uniform with red stripes down the sleeves. He was waving to them to come ashore. By this time, the water was so still that Babette, Barnaby, and Bridget managed to paddle in with their hands.

The soldier, or whatever he was, helped them out, and Bridget retrieved her gum.

"It's a good thing we saw you in time to shut off the dam," said the man. Barnaby looked very satisfied with himself. The man smiled and continued, "You're late, you know. I'd better get you into your uniforms and get you caught up."

"Late for what?" asked Bridget. "Where are we?"

"Hmmm," said the soldier, looking puzzled. "No one comes here accidentally. You either want to be here or . . . or you *have* to be here. I see, I see. Well, either way, you need to change into your uniforms."

"Wait a minute," Bridget protested. "Where are we? Who are you?"

"I'm sorry. My name is Captain Lucid. You are at Fort Report, where we train young cadets like yourselves to write great reports and term papers so we can keep the general informed."

"Informed of what?" asked Babette.

"Informed of anything and everything," replied the captain. "All generals need to be informed."

And with that, he whisked them away to a long, single-story building where the kids outfitted in plain blue uniforms. (Beauregard managed to escape this by hissing, frightening the soldier who was trying to measure him.) A few minutes later, they were all sitting in the great hall of the fort's main building. They were the only ones in the giant lecture hall, but Captain Lucid, who stood at the head of the room, was talking loudly, as if it were filled with hundreds of people.

"Good reports and term papers begin with good research," he began. "You must be familiar with your topic, whatever it may be. One important skill you must possess is knowing how to find your way around a library. You may want to take notes."

Beauregard says librarians are nice. When you go to a library for the first time, it's easy to get confused because you don't know where things are. Don't get frustrated! You can save yourself a whole bunch of trouble by just going to the main desk and asking if a librarian can give you a tour.

Likewise, if you are having trouble finding information on a certain topic, ask a librarian. Librarians are specially trained to find information and are there to help you.

WHAT YOU'LL FIND IN A LIBRARY

Books—Well, obviously you'll find books. That's what libraries are famous for. You'll find books on all sorts of topics, fiction and nonfiction, written by all sorts of people. If you want a treat, have someone take you to your town's public library or to the library at a local college. You'll find books on topics you've never even heard of—shelf after shelf after shelf of them.

References—Reference books are books, of course, but they are kept separate from the rest of the books in the library, in the reference section. This section includes encyclopedias, dictionaries, and almanacs. You are not allowed to check these books out or take them out of the building.

Periodicals—Periodicals are magazines, newspapers, and journals—anything that is published periodically, which means every so often, like once a week or once a month. Libraries usually subscribe to many periodicals that deal with a variety of subjects. Periodicals are useful because they often contain more up-to-date information than do books.

If you want to see if there are any magazine or journal articles on a topic you are researching, ask the librarian for the *Reader's Guide to Periodical Literature*. This is a reference book that lists articles alphabetically by topic. Recent copies of periodicals are usually kept on the library shelves, but older copies are stored on . . .

Microfilm/Microfiche—Old newspapers, magazines, and journals take up a lot of room, so most of them are transferred to microfilm or microfiche. Basically, pictures of the pages are taken and shrunk very small, so that hundreds of pages can be stored in a little case. To read the microfilm, you have to put it in a special light machine that projects the pictures so they are big enough for you to read.

Computers/CD-ROM—Computers are part of our daily lives. CD-ROMs are compact discs that can store volumes of information that can be read by a computer. (The discs are just like the ones that have music on them.) Some CD-ROMs can store an atlas of the whole world or even an entire set of encyclopedias. Most libraries have computers and CD-ROMs available for people to use. Ask your librarian about these resources at your library.

Other Stuff—Some libraries have special sections with music recordings, videos, filmstrips, rare books, and other things.

✎ ✎ ✎ ✎ ✎

Bridget, Babette, and Barnaby scribbled notes furiously. Beauregard slept.

"Is everybody with me so far?" asked Captain Lucid.

Babette shook her hand out by her side, trying to get rid of a cramp. "Yes, I understand what kinds of information are available," she said. "But libraries are so large. How do I find what I need without searching everywhere?"

"I'm glad you asked," said the soldier. "Luckily, libraries are pretty clearly mapped out. All you need to do is understand the map. Let me explain."

Finding What You Need in a Library

Classification

Dewey Decimal System—Back in the late 1800s a librarian named Melvil Dewey came up with a system for assigning number codes to *nonfiction* books. There are ten major categories.

000–099 General Works

100–199 Philosophy and Psychology

200–299 Religion

300–399 Social Science

400–499 Language

500–599 Science and Mathematics

600–699 Technology

700–799 The Arts

800–899 Literature

900–999 History and Geography

Within each category there are many narrower categories that have their own numbers—for example, public performances go under 791. Within each narrow category the books are arranged alphabetically by the author's last name.

At libraries using the Dewey Decimal System the shelves will be clearly marked with the numbers they contain, and the spines of the books will be marked with their numbers. Works of *fiction*, such as novels and short-story collections, will be in a section marked "Fiction" and stacked alphabetically by the author's last name. Biographies—books about people's lives—are usually marked with a "B" and stacked separately.

Library of Congress Classification—Many larger libraries use the Library of Congress classification system to keep track of their materials. The LC system uses letters of the alphabet to form twenty-one broad categories, then narrows down the categories by adding second letters and numbers.

Each book has its own LC number, which will be the same no matter what library you go to. You can find this number listed inside most American books, printed near the beginning on the copyright page. For example, the novel *The Neon Bible* by John Kennedy Toole is marked PS 3570.O54N46 1989. Sure, it's a long number, but no other book has the same one.

In libraries that use the LC system books are grouped alphabetically by letter first and then by number within each category; for example, PA 3245 would come before PZ 071. The shelves and the books will be clearly marked.

Your Road Map: The Card Catalog

The **card catalog** is a big cabinet full of drawers containing alphabetically arranged cards. Each card has a **call number** listed on it in the upper left-hand corner. The call number will be either the Dewey Decimal number or the Library of Congress number.

Once you have the call number, it's easy to find the book you want. Most libraries have maps showing how their books are stacked. Go to the map, find where your call number would fit in, and go get the book! If you run into trouble, ask a librarian.

For each book the card catalog contains three different kinds of cards: **author, title,** and **subject.**

- **Author cards**—You can look up a book by the author's last name. For instance, if someone told you that you would enjoy a book by S. E. Hinton but you don't remember the title, you could go to the "H" drawer of the card catalog and look up "Hinton." All the books the library has by S. E. Hinton will have cards.

- **Title cards**—If you remember only the title of a book like *The Outsiders,* you can look it up too. Ignore any beginning article (the words *A, An,* or *The*) and look up the book by the first letter of the first word in the title; in this case "O" for *Outsiders.*

- **Subject cards**—Let's say you are just beginning to do research on a topic and you don't know the names of any books or authors that might help you. You can look up your topic alphabetically, but start with a *broad* topic and then try to narrow it down. If your topic is "trapeze artists in Europe during the 1800s," you might start with the word *circus* instead of *trapeze.* If your topic is "the development of special effects in film," you would probably try *film* instead of *special effects.*

Don't get frustrated if you can't find the topic you want right away. *Ask the librarian for help.*

Most cards contain publication information (like when the book was published and the name of the publisher) and a brief description of what the book is about. Card catalogs also contain **cross-reference cards.** These are sometimes called "see also" cards, because they read "See also . . ." or "See . . ." and refer you to another topic. For example, if you are looking under the topic "pottery," there might be a card that reads "See also: porcelain," because porcelain is a closely related topic.

Cross-reference cards also steer you in the right direction. You might be trying to look up information on the planet Saturn under "Saturn," and you might find a card that says "See: solar system." That means that books on Saturn are listed under the subject "solar system."

Remember: If you want to see if there are any articles in periodicals that might help you, look in the reference section for the *Reader's Guide to Periodical Literature.*

- **Computerized catalogs**—Many libraries use computerized catalogs. Some haven't completely done away with their old cabinets of cards, but it's likely that there is a library in your town that has computer terminals to help you look things up. Most of these computers work like the old card system—you can look things up by author, title, or subject. On some computers you can look up books and periodicals. Sometimes, there are certain computers for books and others for periodicals. These computers are usually very easy to use. There are instructions to walk you through the program but, as always, ask for help if you need it.

- **Online computer sources**—If you have access to a computer and a modem, you can get on the Internet and gather information on an almost limitless variety of topics using search engines. Some of the most popular and useful search engines are Yahoo!, Google, Excite, and Ask Jeeves. All you have to do is go to the search engine's website, type in your topic, and then you'll see a list of websites that contain information about the topic you searched for. Some of these websites will be more useful than others, so look through a bunch of them before you decide which ones to use for your research.

(See pages 269–280 for more information about computers and writing.)

✎ ✎ ✎ ✎ ✎

"Now then," announced Captain Lucid. "Let's see if you've been paying attention. Try answering the following questions."

✍ QUIZ #5 ✍
Looking into Libraries

1. What are the two main systems for organizing books in a library?

   _____

   _____

   _____

   _____

2. List the four kinds of cards you'll find in a card catalog.

   _____

   _____

   _____

   _____

   _____

Bonus: Name the inventor of one of these systems.

_____

_____

3. When looking at a card from the card catalog, where would you find the call number?
   (a) Upper right-hand corner
   (b) Lower right-hand corner
   (c) Upper left-hand corner
   (d) Lower left-hand corner

4. List three examples of periodicals.

_____

_____

_____

_____

5. What are two ways periodicals are stored in a library?

_____

_____

_____

Chapter 5
A Bunch of Grunts in Basic Training

Barnaby looked terribly excited about what he'd just learned. "I never realized it was so easy to get information," he cried. "I'm ready to get going. Let's start writing some reports!" He leaped up from his seat, pen in hand, as if he were ready to charge into battle.

"Oh no you don't!" said the Captain, chuckling. "All you know is how to use the resources available to you. You have the supplies, but you don't know what to do with them. We haven't even *started* basic training yet!"

Bridget gulped. "This sounds like it's going to be hard."

"Well, let's face it, writing reports is not something most people do for fun on the weekends," replied the Captain. "But you have to learn, and I'm going to teach you. By the time I'm done, you'll all be lean, mean *report-writing machines!*"

"Sounds very glamorous," Babette commented, but Captain Lucid didn't hear. He had already begun talking.

"Attention!" he barked. "Prepare to be trained. First, let's define our terms."

If your teachers ask you to write **reports**, they want something factual. Reports can also be called *descriptive essays*. A report is like a detailed, clear explanation of something. You find out the facts and then organize them and write them out. You've probably already had to do this at school.

A **paper,** or term paper, on the other hand, is more of an analysis than a factual report. It also can be called a *persuasive essay*. If teachers assign papers, they want you to *think critically* about a topic and say what *your* opinions are on the subject. That doesn't mean you can just rave on and on about what you like and don't like. You have to do research and support what you say with facts and examples, but if you give nothing but the facts, you probably won't get a very good grade. You will have to draw conclusions and make judgments.

You probably won't have to write a term paper like this until high school, but writing reports now gives you good practice using the kinds of skills you will need when the time comes. The further you go in school, the more you will be expected to come up with original ideas and write about them convincingly. In the meantime we're going to focus on reports that require research.

REPORTS THAT RULE

Selecting a Topic

Picking a topic for a report can be one of the most difficult parts of the writing process. Thinking through your topic ahead of time will save you a whole lot of trouble later, though. Here's how to do it.

Length and Depth

Suppose your teacher asks you to write a five-page paper dealing with the Native American tribes of Central and South America. The first thing you must do is *think of your limits*. You have five pages. If you wanted to talk about every tribe in Central and South

America, you could only mention the most general details about each. This is a *very broad* topic. You would only have room for a couple of sentences on each tribe. That's okay, if that's what you want. However, overly broad and general papers usually aren't very interesting.

If you wanted to limit your discussion to one tribe, you could go into a little more detail. But even this is a **broad** topic. You could talk about the area in which they lived, their religious customs, their housing, or their food. But, again, you wouldn't have room for more than a couple of paragraphs on each of these subjects.

But suppose you got even more specific. What if you decided to write about the accuracy of the calendar designed by the Maya, a tribe that lived in what is now Mexico, Guatemala, and Belize? This is a *narrow* topic. You could go into quite a lot of detail. You could explain what is known about how the Maya made their calendar, what some of its faults were, what some of its strong points were, and how it compares to our own calendar.

The point is that you should think about your space limits and about what you want to accomplish. If you haven't thought your topic through, your report won't turn out very well. The following are some problems you could run into:

A topic that's too broad—If your topic is too broad for the assigned length of the report, your report will probably wind up reading like a bunch of unrelated facts all thrown together or like general statements with no supporting evidence. Usually, halfway through writing such a report, you'll realize that there's no way you can include all the information you need to explain everything. But by then, it may be too late to do anything about it. This is the most common problem with student reports.

An example would be deciding to write a five-page report on the Crusades of the Middle Ages. The Crusades were a series of invasions by Christians against non-Christians, primarily in North Africa and the Middle East. They continued for hundreds of years and had serious religious and political effects. You could barely touch the surface of this topic in five pages—volumes have been written on it.

A topic that's too narrow—It's also possible that your topic is so specific that you can't find enough information to satisfy the page requirement. Reports that have too narrow a focus usually wind up repeating themselves in order to fill up space. It doesn't happen often, but it does happen, especially on longer reports.

An example would be deciding to write a twenty-page report on how water turns to steam. You could give a perfectly good, very detailed explanation of how water turns to steam—and even include a picture or two—in fewer than ten pages.

So your mission is to keep the length of your report balanced with the depth and to pick a topic that lets you do that. Now that we're clear on that, let's see *how*.

The Five-W and One-H Technique

Your teacher almost always, will give you a general topic on which to write a report. Let's say the topic is the country of Indonesia. Even if you know very little about the topic, the "Five-W and One-H" technique can help you get a handle on it.

The five Ws and one H refer to those handy question words: *who, what, where, when, why,* and their cousin, *how.* To use them, get a sheet of paper and start writing down questions you have about Indonesia. Use these question words to ask questions about the topic. Try to use all the question words and be as specific as possible. Here's how.

Where is Indonesia located?

What are the main religions of Indonesia?

Who were the first Europeans to visit Indonesia?

Who inhabited Indonesia before the arrival of the Europeans?

How have Europeans affected Indonesia?

What are the main industries in Indonesia?

How many islands are in Indonesia?

What is the most densely populated island?

When did Indonesia become an independent nation?

When was the last war in Indonesia fought?

Why did Indonesia fight this war?

Do any of these questions interest you? Pick one that does and use it as a springboard for your research. By going through this process, you gain focus and cut down on your research time because you'll go to the library knowing pretty much what you're looking for.

Narrowing it down—The more you know about the topic ahead of time, the easier it is to pick a final topic *before* going to the library, but you still might have to narrow down your topic more. Say, for example, you decided to focus on the question, "Who inhabited Indonesia before the arrival of the Europeans?" After doing a little research on this topic, you'd find out about the Srivijaya empire that started back in the seventh century, the Mataram kingdom in Java, and the powerful Majapahit empire that controlled several islands. If you decide you're most interested in the Majapahit empire, start the whole Five-W, One-H technique again:

> When did the Majapahit empire rise to power?
>
> Why does it no longer exist?
>
> How long did the Majapahit empire last?
>
> Who is considered the greatest Majapahit ruler and why?
>
> What contributions did the Majapahit make to Indonesian culture?
>
> Where did the Majapahit come from?

Keep repeating the process until you have a topic you can handle in the assigned length of your report.

Many people think better with pictures than with words. If you're one of those people, try one of the following methods for coming up with report ideas.

Tree Charts

Tree charts can be used for many things, from helping you organize complicated tasks to clarifying concepts that confuse you in school. They are also helpful in coming up with good ideas for reports. Not all topics lend themselves to this technique, so use it only if it seems easy and useful.

Tree charts, as the name suggests, are based on the concept of a tree: trunks, limbs, branches, smaller branches, twigs, leaves, and roots. Let's say the general topic for your report is U.S. presidents. To start narrowing the topic, get a piece of paper, draw a "trunk" in the middle of it, and write "U.S. presidents" next to it.

Now let's think about the large limbs. How would you break down the subject "U.S. presidents"? It makes sense to make each big limb the name of a president, doesn't it? But don't worry—you don't have to write down all of them. Just make limbs for the ones you know and think are interesting. Let's say you choose Thomas Jefferson, Ulysses S. Grant, Woodrow Wilson, and Richard Nixon.

Off each limb come smaller branches. For each of the presidents you chose, think of what they were known for and what was going on when they were president, and make branches for those ideas and events. You'd probably wind up with something like this.

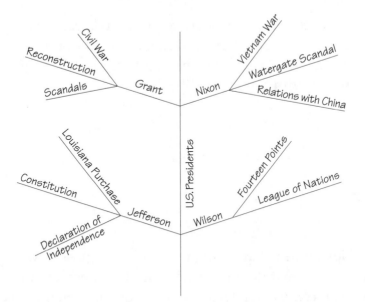

Pick one of the branches as the starting point for your research. After you know a little more about your topic, you can repeat the "tree-drawing" process, but this time use the name of the branch—say, "Jefferson and the Louisiana Purchase"—as your trunk. Break down the topic into limbs and branches until you have a topic you feel you can cover thoroughly in the space you've been allowed.

Cluster Charts

Cluster charts are a lot like tree charts, but they give you a little more freedom to go off in any direction you choose. To start a cluster chart, take the general topic ("let's say it's baseball this time)," write it down in the middle of a piece of paper, and put a circle around it.

Now start thinking about anything you can that relates to baseball, write it down in a circle, and connect that circle to the "baseball" circle. You might wind up with something like this.

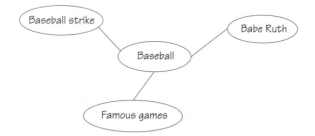

Next, think of anything that relates to those new topics, write it down in a circle, and connect it to the topic it came from. Here's what your chart might look like now:

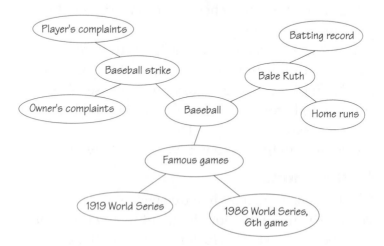

Depending on the length of the report you've been assigned, either some of the first set of circles you made or some of the second set will be good starting points. Pick a starting point and head off to the library.

BRAINSTORMING

If you can get together with a friend or a few friends from your class, another way to come up with topics is to "brainstorm." Brainstorming is even more free-form than clustering. You and your friends say whatever you can think of that relates to the general topic and write down the ideas on a piece of paper. Don't decide whether the ideas are good or bad right then. The point is to keep an open mind and say whatever you think of. Usually, a group of three or four people works best because other people's ideas will help you come up with more ideas, and your ideas will help them.

Just keep writing down every idea until you think you've done enough. These ideas often need to be narrowed down, but brainstorming is a fun way to come up with fresh and new topics.

✎ ✎ ✎ ✎ ✎

"You must be careful when selecting a topic, I see," said Babette, thoughtfully.

"Yes," said Captain Lucid. "But the more thinking and planning you do early on, the easier and stronger your report will be. All that effort pays off, believe me."

"We do, we do," said Bridget, somewhat impatiently. "What comes next? Can we start writing now?"

"No, I'm afraid that's a ways off yet," the Captain replied. "There are a couple of other matters to cover first—like research techniques."

RESEARCH WITHOUT TEARS

Well, maybe you wouldn't have cried during your research, but many people do become very frustrated. But if you approach the task with the right supplies and the right strategy, it should be kind of fun. All you need to start out are paper, pens, and a packet of small index cards. You'll find out why in a minute.

Beauregard says the research methods you'll learn here can be used for the longest reports or papers you'll ever have to write—even if you have to write a hundred pages on a topic. If the report you have to write is only one or two pages long, though, you might find the process we're about to describe a bit too complicated. If so, trim down some of the steps, but on anything longer than five pages, you'll be miles ahead if you go through the whole process step by step.

Skimming and Pre-reading

You already know how to look things up in the library. Go to the card catalog, copy down the titles and call numbers of any books on your topic that look interesting, pull as many as you can off the shelves, and then find yourself a desk or table to sit at.

It's time to make yourself more familiar with your topic. Look through the tables of contents, skim through some of the chapters, and stop to read carefully anything that catches your eye. Keep reading until you feel comfortable enough with your topic that you think you could have a conversation about it.

If you still need to narrow down your topic, use one of the techniques—Five-W and One-H, tree charts, or cluster charts—we discussed before. Otherwise . . .

Write Your Summary Sentence

Before you begin your serious research and before you begin writing, it's a good idea to know exactly what your mission is. The best way to define your mission is with a summary sentence. The summary sentence should be one sentence that states the entire purpose of your report. You can use this sentence as the first sentence of your report if you want, but it is not necessary. It is mainly a tool to keep you focused during your research.

Summary sentences are not titles and are not vague. Here are a few examples.

- Doctors have used leeches for medicinal purposes for thousands of years—during ancient times to release "evil spirits," during the Middle Ages and Renaissance to balance the "four humors," and even today to reduce swelling and prevent blood clots.

- Hercules, the son of the Greek god Zeus, was forced to do penance for killing his wife and children by serving the Argive king, who gave him twelve dangerous, difficult tasks to complete to free himself from punishment.

- In the seventeenth century, French Protestants known as Huguenots left France to escape persecution, often coming to American colonies, where many became prominent and wealthy.

Imagine that you are trying to summarize your report in one sentence. That would be your summary sentence. If you have trouble performing this task, you might not know enough about your topic yet. Keep reading until you can write your summary sentence.

Make an Outline

Outlines are short sketches. They can be very broad or very specific. They will save you a lot of time during your research. Here's the traditional way to do an outline. First, decide what the main points of your report will be. Say we picked the "medicinal uses of leeches" topic above. Our main points could be: ancient medicinal uses of leeches, medieval uses of leeches, Renaissance uses of leeches, famous people who were treated with leeches, and modern medicinal uses of leeches. You'd also want to leave room for an introduction and a conclusion. Using Roman numerals, we'd write them out like this.

I.   Introduction

II. Ancient medicinal uses of leeches

III. Medieval uses of leeches

IV. Renaissance uses of leeches

V.   Famous people who were treated with leeches

VI. Modern medicinal uses of leeches

VII. Conclusion

Make sure these are the broader points of your report. You should plan to write at least a paragraph on each of these topics. If you can't, it's not important enough to have it's own heading and you should put it under another heading.

Beauregard says Roman numerals were the numbers used by the ancient Romans. We still use them for various reasons today. In case you've never seen or used them before, here's a list of the numbers one through ten: I, II, III, IV, V, VI, VII, VIII, IX, X.

Next, break down each broad point into smaller points and write them under the broader points using capital letters to set them off. If you have even smaller points under these points, set them off with regular Arabic numerals:

I. Introduction

II. Ancient medicinal uses of leeches

    A. Use in the Far East

    B. Greek use to release evil spirits

III. Medieval uses of leeches

    A. Four humors of the body

    B. Use by barbers/doctors

IV. Renaissance uses of leeches

    A. Popularity in Europe

        1. Skyrocketing demand

        2. Near extinction of medicinal leech

    B. Dr. Broussais's theory of swelling of digestive tract

C. Other uses

    1. Black eyes

    2. Varicose veins

    3. Headaches

V. Famous people who were treated with leeches

    A. George Washington

    B. Adolf Hitler

    C. Joseph Stalin

VI. Modern medicinal uses of leeches

    A. Reattachment of severed body parts

    B. Skin grafts

    C. Reduction of swelling

VII. Conclusion

If you wanted to go even further with your outline, you could use lowercase letters under the Arabic numerals, and after that use little Roman numerals (i, ii, iii, iv, v) under the lowercase letters.

Try to put as much information as you can into your outline. The more detailed it is, the easier it will be for you to write your report.

Gathering and Organizing Information

Here's where those index cards come into play. First, decide which books you are going to use. For each book, pull out an index card.

On each index card, write

- the author's name (last name, then first name)
- the title (underlined)
- what city the book was published in
- the name of the publisher
- the copyright date

You can find this information on what's called the copyright page, which is usually the second or fourth page of a book. The copyright date is the date the book was published, and it is set off with the symbol ©.

Next, make a symbol of some sort, like a star or circle or squiggle, in the upper right-hand corner. If you have colored pens or pencils, you can give each book card it's own color code by making different-colored dots in the corners. Either way is fine, as long as each book card has its own special mark. Your card might look something like this.

~

Delaney, Frank. <u>Legends of the Celts</u>
New York, NY. Sterling Publishing Company, 1989.

Make a card like this for every book or magazine you intend to take information from and then put the cards aside.

Beauregard says last-minute tweaks are okay. As you get into serious research on your topic, you may learn something new about it that you really want to include in your report, or you may learn that your outline and summary sentence are off the mark in some way. That happens to the best of us. It is important to go back and make adjustments to your outline and summary sentence as soon as you realize there's a problem. Don't wait until you finish your research, or you'll be in a heap of trouble.

Now, with your outline and summary sentence handy, start going through your sources. Every time you see a piece of information, a fact, a quotation, or anything that fits into your outline, take out an index card and write down that information—word for word, if necessary. Write the page number or numbers on the card and, in the upper right-hand corner, *write the symbol you assigned to that book.*

Make a card for every piece of information you want to include. By writing down the symbols and page numbers on the card, you'll always know where the information came from, and at the end of your report, when you have to write a list of sources, you'll know right away which books you used.

One of your cards might look like this.

~

> Ireland never came fully under the influence of the Romans, so it preserved the culture and history of the Celts for hundreds of years after the birth of Christ. p. 1.

Be careful! You shouldn't be writing down everything you see—only exact facts, dates, quotations, and interesting pieces of information. You don't have to copy the entire book onto index cards.

After you've gone through your sources thoroughly, put the books aside, pull out your outline, and begin arranging your index cards according to the outline. Mark the back of the index card with the section of the outline in which it belongs. For example, going back to our outline on "the medicinal uses of leeches," you would pull any index cards that have information on "the four humors" and mark them "III.A," and you would mark any with information on "barbers/doctors" as "III.B." That way, if the cards get mixed up, you can easily put them back in order.

✎ ✎ ✎ ✎ ✎

"That seems like a whole lot of work," said Bridget. "And we haven't even started writing yet." She eyed Beauregard, who was slowly stretching himself out before curling back into a sleepy ball, enviously.

"It just seems that way the first time you try it," Captain Lucid replied. "The more reports you write, the easier it gets. And you'll be glad you have good research and organization habits. They'll save you a lot of heartache."

"Excuse me for interrupting, Captain, but is it time to start writing yet?" asked Barnaby, clutching his pen eagerly.

"Why, yes," smiled the Captain. "In fact, it is time. Get out your index cards. Let's talk about writing. First, I want to give you a Rule that will serve you well on all writing projects. . . ."

"Did he say 'Rule'?" asked Babette. "Aren't we supposed to learn these Rules?"

"And that Rule is . . . " continued the Captain.

"Quick! Write this down!" urged Babette.

RULE #2
Clear writing demands clear thinking.

"That's right," said the Captain. "And muddled heads make muddled writing. Always keep in mind what you are trying to accomplish."

REPORT WRITING THE RIGHT WAY

Having clear thoughts on your topic is *so* important that it bears saying one more time: *Think things through! Clear writing demands clear thinking!* Got it? Are you sure?

Shut yourself in a room with no distractions—no stereo, no television (not even turned all the way down), no unnecessary people, and even no windows, if possible. If you're going to create the report on a computer, open a new document. If you're going to write or type it, get a notebook or several sheets of paper. Get your index cards. Take some cleansing breaths. Ready?

Well, good, but there are a few notes on paragraph structure we should get out of the way first.

Statement/Support Paragraphs

In statement/support paragraphs, open with a statement of fact or opinion and then give supporting details. Read the following example:

> The area known as the south pole on the continent of Antarctica is uninhabitable by humans. Temperatures rarely climb above 0 degrees Fahrenheit, even in the summer, and often plunge below –50 degrees. Blizzard-force winds ravage the land, making it hard to build any lasting structures. In addition to these climatic difficulties, there are few natural sources of food on the continent. Since there are no supermarkets or restaurants, either, it's likely that humans would starve to death if they didn't freeze to death first.

See how every sentence supports the opening statement?

Chronological or Time-Ordered Paragraphs

The word *chronological* means "ordered by time." Sometimes it's easiest to present your facts in this order, especially if you are describing an event or process. Here is an example.

> The infielders' performances at last night's softball game were superb, especially the triple play that ended the ninth inning. With runners at first and second, Camino, batting for the Yellow Jackets, knocked a grounder to third base. Petri, the third baseman, scooped up the ball, tagged his base, and

gunned the ball to Sheehan at second, thereby getting both base runners out. Sheehan would not be satisfied with a double play, it seemed. With what can only be called lightning speed, he zipped the ball to first, ending not only the game, but any hope the Yellow Jackets had for a playoff spot.

Spatial Order Paragraphs

Arranging a paragraph in spatial order works well if you are describing a scene, a room, or other location. You present things in order of their appearance. For example

The new music club and restaurant, Eat to the Beat, had everything it needed to be a success. In the back, there was a stage large enough for a small orchestra, and right in front of it, tables for groups of two to six were arranged with great views of the entertainment. Farther away from the stage, closer to the entrance, both large and small tables were set for people who preferred to have the music in the background. Just to the left of the entrance was a long, oak bar stocked with the finest beverages. Unfortunately, despite such features, the club went down the tubes within a month.

Compare and Contrast Paragraphs

In this type of paragraph, you list the similarities and differences between two things. Here is an example.

> Country music and blues music may seem like opposites, but actually they have many things in common. For example, most old country songs, just like traditional blues songs, are written about separation, loss, and heartache, or, on the happier side, going out and having a good time. Musically, country and blues share similar eight-bar or twelve-bar chord structures, but country has a much boxier beat when compared to the steady, driving rhythm of blues songs. While both country and the blues influenced the development of rock 'n' roll, blues proved a more fertile source, giving birth to jazz, be-bop, fusion, disco, rap, and funk.

Of course, these aren't the only ways to organize a paragraph, but they are good models. If writing a paragraph comes naturally to you, you probably won't even have to think much about structure. If you get stuck, though, see if one of these models might help you. Okay, now it's really time to start writing, so pick up that pen and let's go. . . .

STEP 1: Link them up

The first thing you need to do is forget about the introduction. It's almost always easier to write the introduction *after* you've finished the paper. That way, you know what you're introducing.

Now gather the index cards for your first major section. Make sure they are in the order in which you want to present the information. Read them over a few times and think about how you'd explain things in your own words. Then start writing sentences and paragraphs that link up all those pieces of information. When you've included all the information, stop. Gather your cards for the next section and repeat the process. Keep going until you've gone through your entire outline.

After you've written the body, go back and write the **introductory paragraph.** Remember, you can use your summary sentence as the first sentence if you want. The introductory paragraph should catch your readers' interest and set the stage for the rest of the report. Basically, all you have to do is prepare readers for the report by telling them what to expect.

The conclusion of your report should be short and sweet. Just sum up your main points. It's that simple.

You're probably thinking, "Wait a minute. After all that preparation, all I have to do is link up our index cards?" Pretty much, yes. You'll have to work out some kinks, but once you're done with step 1, you'll have what's called a **rough draft.**

 **Beauregard says** skipping lines saves time. If you are writing your report out by hand, try skipping a line or two between each one you write. That way, if you want to go back and make additions or corrections, you'll have room to write in and your draft won't get all jumbled and messed up.

STEP 2: Smooth it out

When you've finished your rough draft, take a little break. Have a snack. Play a video game. Do something you enjoy. You deserve it—you're done with the hardest part. (Don't forget to come back, though—you're not quite finished yet.)

When you come back, read your draft as if you know nothing about the topic and someone else wrote the report. Be critical—pretend you are your teacher and *look* for things that are wrong. Make corrections and additions as you go. The following are some of the things you should watch out for.

Awkward transitions, clumsy sentences—There is no sure-fire method for writing graceful sentences and making smooth transitions between sentences and paragraphs. The more books, magazines, and newspapers you read, the smoother and more natural your writing will become. Other than saying "read more," the best advice we can give is to *use your ears.* Read what you've written out loud. If it is choppy or confusing, rewrite it.

Here's a list of some of the **transition words and phrases** you can use.

according to	for this reason	next
also	however	on the other hand
although	in addition	second
as a result	in contrast	similarly
because	in fact	since

besides	in particular	so
due to	instead of	such as
during	last	then
finally	likewise	therefore
first	meanwhile	unlike
for example	nevertheless	yet

Other popular techniques for linking sentences and making paragraphs stronger include using **repetition** and **word chains.** Both of these methods have been used by famous speakers and writers since the ancient Greek philosophers, Aristotle and Plato, wrote their works.

With repetition, the same word or phrase is used several times for emphasis and effect. With word chains, a synonym (a word that has the same meaning as another word) or pronoun is used to refer to the same thing or idea throughout a paragraph. Look at the following examples:

Repetition

In a <u>hole</u> in the ground there lived a hobbit. Not a nasty, dirty, wet <u>hole</u>, filled with the ends of worms and an oozy smell, nor yet a dry, bare, sandy <u>hole</u> with nothing in it to sit down on or to eat: it was a hobbit-<u>hole</u>, and that means comfort.

from *The Hobbit,* J.R.R. Tolkien

I <u>speak</u> not to disprove what Brutus <u>spoke</u>,
But here I am to <u>speak</u> what I do know.
You all did love him once, not without <u>cause</u>;

What <u>cause</u> withholds you, then, to mourn
for him?

> from Marc Antony's funeral speech from
> Shakespeare's *Julius Caesar*

. . . we here highly resolve . . . that government
of <u>the people</u>, by <u>the people</u>, for <u>the people</u>, shall
not perish from the earth.

> from Abraham Lincoln's "Gettysburg
> Address" (This is a very famous speech,
> filled with repetition for effect. Ask your
> teacher to show you a complete copy.)

<u>We must all hang</u> together, or assuredly <u>we shall
all hang</u> separately.

> Benjamin Franklin, at the signing of the
> Declaration of Independence

Nonviolence is the answer to the crucial political
and moral questions of our time; the need for man
to overcome <u>oppression and violence</u> without
resorting to <u>oppression and violence</u>.

> Dr. Martin Luther King Jr., in his speech
> accepting the Nobel Peace Prize

Word chains

A <u>spider's web</u> is stronger than <u>it</u> looks. Although
<u>it</u> is made of thin, delicate strands, the <u>web</u> is not
easily broken. However, a <u>web</u> gets torn every day
by the insects that kick around in <u>it</u>, and a spider
must rebuild <u>it</u> when <u>it</u> gets full of holes.

> from *Charlotte's Web*, E. B. White

Then she became aware of the spectacle she presented to their surprised vision: <u>roses</u> at her breast; <u>roses</u> in her hat; <u>roses</u> and strawberries in her basket to the brim. She blushed and said confusedly that the <u>flowers</u> had been given to her. When the passengers were not looking she stealthily removed the more prominent <u>blooms</u> from her hat and placed <u>them</u> in the basket, where she covered <u>them</u> with her handkerchief.

from *Tess of the d'Urbervilles*, Thomas Hardy

On the wall, gleaming, he spied a tremendous <u>sword</u> (by giants of olden time forged in the furnace of the sun), undimmed in luster, so cumbersome only a hero could wield <u>it</u>. He grabbed the <u>golden hilt</u> and, wheeling mightily, smote with all his strength. Splintering her bone-rings, the <u>blade</u> hacked through her neck and felled her at his feet, stone dead. Then great Beowulf rejoiced. Fierce as the summer sun blazed the <u>steel</u> in his hand, a beacon of brightness lighting the way.

from *Beowulf,* an ancient tale of heroism

Beauregard says repetition for effect is like perfume—a little goes a long way. Don't use this technique too much or your readers will be turned off. Repetition also is a good technique only when you do it on purpose. If you just use the same word over and over again because you can't think of another one, that's not repetition for effect—that's boring. Get a thesaurus, which is a book of synonyms, and spice up your writing!

Grammar and spelling—Your report may be full of great facts and ideas, but if it's also full of grammar and spelling errors, few people will notice all the interesting information you've gathered. Nothing ruins a good report more easily than does careless errors.

If you're working on a computer, you're in luck. Most word-processing programs have a built-in spell-checker, which you should definitely use. Don't think, however, that this means you don't have to check your work. Computers can't do everything. If you're writing in a notebook, get yourself a good dictionary and look up any words you're not sure about. Even professional writers keep dictionaries handy.

If you feel a little shaky on the finer points of grammar, it's a good idea to ask someone whose grammar skills you trust to read through your report and make suggestions. This could be your mother or father, an older brother or sister, or even a classmate.

Forgetting to use paragraphs—Remember that paragraphs make your writing clearer and easier to read. Try not to write more than a page without starting a new paragraph.

Beauregard says book reports don't usually require library research—you just have to read the assigned book. For a book report, teachers want a clear summary of the plot, as well as descriptions of the setting and main characters. They are mainly interested in whether or not you read and understood the book. That doesn't mean your report can be sloppy and confusing. To write a good book report, you'd follow many of the same steps you would for a research report, but you'd skip some too. Here's how.

- Step 1: Write a summary sentence. See pages 85–86. To write a summary sentence for a book report, ask yourself, "What is this book about?" and answer it in one clear sentence.

- Step 2: Write an outline. See pages 87–89. If you have trouble deciding what the main points are, ask yourself the following questions: What were the most exciting parts of the book? What were the turning points or events in the story that caused big changes in the lives of the characters?

- Step 3: Write a rough draft. This will be easy if you make your outline as detailed as you can. Try to use examples and events from the book to make your report interesting.

- Step 4: Smooth out your book report. Check for clumsy sentences, incorrect spelling and grammar, and paragraph breaks. After you've revised your book report, type or write it out neatly. Then you're all done!

STEP 3: Fit the format

Most teachers, especially in high school and college, require you to present your reports in a standard format, or "style." If your teacher gives you guidelines, follow them exactly. Some teachers, however, will just refer you to a common **style manual,** such as the *MLA Handbook* or *Kate L. Turabian's Manual of Style.* These books explain how to format every piece of writing you can think of—footnotes, endnotes, epigraphs, and quotations of every kind. You probably don't have to worry about all those details just yet, but that doesn't mean your reports shouldn't be neatly formatted. The following are the basics:

Cover sheets: A smart addition or a waste of time?—You've probably seen it before: Your classmate hands in a report with one of those fancy plastic bindings around it. On the front is a brilliant drawing of a lizard that looks like it took hours to create, and in fancy script the title "Our Reptile Friends—by Mark Townsend." You may have even done something like this yourself. After all, it's pretty impressive, right? Teachers are probably so dazzled by the cover that they won't even bother reading the report, or at the very least, they'll look favorably at the report, right? Wrong.

Fancy bindings, folders, and cover decorations do you very little good. In fact, they just make it harder for teachers to carry the reports home, and even the fanciest cover won't distract them from what's inside. If you have time and you like drawing and decorating, go ahead. But remember, art only counts in art class, and your time might be better spent smoothing out your sentences and checking your grammar.

Beauregard says chill out on the fonts. If you have a computer, you're lucky. It may have hundreds of different, cool fonts and type sizes that are fun to fool around with. Don't fool around on your report, though. Now's not the time to try out Heavy Black Gothic or Narrow Helsinki Sans-serif. Stick with Times, Times New Roman, Courier, or another clear, standard font in either 10-point or 12-point size. Weird fonts are hard to read, and too many different fonts on a page can get really annoying.

The first page—Whether you're working on a computer, typing, or writing out your report by hand, the format should be the same. On a standard 8 1/2 × 11-inch piece of paper, set your **margins.** A margin is like an invisible line you won't write past. For your report, your margins on the left and right sides of the page should be set 1 1/4 inches in from the edges. At the top and bottom of the page, the margins should be 1 inch. (On a computer or typewriter, you can set these margins ahead of time. If you're writing your report by hand, you can estimate the margins.)

Your report should be **double spaced** to make it easy to read and to give your teacher room for comments. (Again, on a computer or typewriter, you can adjust for double spacing ahead of time. If you're writing by hand, just skip a space between lines.)

One inch down from the top, right up against the left margin, write your first and last name. Under that, write your teacher's name. Under that, write the name of the class (example: Third Period English). And under that, write the full date.

After you write the date, go down to the next line and, in the center of the page, write the title of your paper. You don't have to put quotes around it or underline it. Just write it, remembering to **capitalize key words in the title**, such as nouns, verbs, adjectives, and adverbs. Words like *and, of, the, a*, and *an* are not capitalized unless they are the first word in the title.

Once you've written the title, skip two spaces (technically four spaces, since you're double spacing), **indent five spaces** from the left and begin your first paragraph. Throughout your whole report, you will indent the first line of every paragraph.

There is no need to put a page number on the first page of your report. In the rest of the report, write your last name and the page number in the upper right-hand corner, a half inch from the top edge of the page (for example, Brighton 4).

Here's how your first page might look:

Sal Paolo
Ms. Kingston
Fourth Period English
December 1, 2002

Black Death:
The Plague That Killed One-Quarter of Europe

_____
_____
_____
_____
_____
_____
_____
_____
_____
_____
_____
_____
_____
_____

Quotations and credits—You have to give credit where credit is due. In a report that means

acknowledging your sources. If you include a direct, word-for-word quote from a book or article, you must put quotation marks around it, even if it's only four or five words. If you don't, it's called **plagiarism,** which is like stealing. It's also plagiarism to take another person's idea, even if you put it in your own words. There are a few ways to give credit to your source, but the easiest is the **parenthetical method.** At the end of the sentence in which you quote or use an idea from a book or article, write in parentheses the last name of the author and the page number the information came from. If you mention the title or the author of the book in the sentence, you don't have to list the author in the parentheses.

Here's how it looks.

> The madness and cruelty of the Roman emperors during the last years of the Empire could be blamed on "weak genes and unchecked authority" (Maccio 142).

> According to William Hogarth in his book *Irish Mist*, "the unusual size, bleached hair, and blood-curdling battle cries" of the ancient Celtic warriors frightened even the strongest armies of the time (54).

> In his famous book on politics, *The Prince*, Machiavelli says that generosity in a ruler is only worthwhile if everyone knows about it, and good deeds done without public knowledge are a harmful waste of time (60).

If you are using more than one book by the same author, put a shortened form of the title of the book in parentheses instead of the author's last name. For example, two books by historian Barbara Tuchman are *A Distant Mirror*, which could be shortened to *Mirror*, and *The Guns of August*, which could be shortened to *Guns*.

The bibliography, or list of works cited—Once you've finished typing or writing your report, you have one last thing to do: provide a list of your sources. On a new piece of paper, start one inch down from the top and write either "Bibliography" or "Works Cited" in the center of the page. Then skip one space.

Remember the index cards you filled out for each book? Here's where they come in handy. If you wrote them the way we showed you, all you have to do is arrange them in alphabetical order by the author's last name. Then list them in the following format (notice that here, the first lines are right up against the left-hand margin, and the second and third lines are indented).

Works Cited

Melville, Herman. <u>Moby Dick</u>. New York:
    Penguin, Inc.,1961.

Pirsig, Robert M. <u>Zen and the Art of
    Motorcycle Maintenance: An Inquiry
    into Values</u>. New York: William Morrow
    and Co., 1974.

Poe, Edgar Allan. <u>Complete Tales and Poems of Edgar Allan Poe</u>. New York: Vintage Books, 1975.

Beauregard says don't get too hung up. The basic rules of formatting a report are covered here, but there are so many different rules on formatting reports, papers, and bibliographies that it would make your head spin. Don't get hung up on it all. You'll have plenty of time to worry about the correct way to cite a live television broadcast or a quote from a translated opera when  you get to college. Just make sure your report is neat, concentrate on your writing skills, and you'll be fine.

✎ ✎ ✎ ✎ ✎

"Congratulations, troops, you've made it through basic report training," Captain Lucid cried enthusiastically. "How do you feel?"

"A little tired, quite frankly," said Babette, stretching her arms above her head.

"Well, the first report is always the hardest," he answered cheerily. "But now that you know how to go about it, you'll never have to be afraid of writing a report or paper again for as long as you're in school."

Babette, Bridget, and Barnaby smiled smugly. "I guess it *is* nice to feel confident about something most people dread," Bridget said.

Beauregard, who had awakened from his nap, appeared to be reading the kids' reports.

"What do you think, um . . . Beauregard is your name, right?" asked the Captain.

Beauregard grinned and then pushed one of the reports toward the Captain, who picked it up and looked it over.

"I see," he said. "You like this one. Well, I certainly see why. I'll share it with the other students so they can see an example of a good, short report."

Barnaby Bain
Captain Lucid
Basic Report Training
February 10, 2002

The Rise and Fall and Rise of
the Popularity of Cats

Since the beginning of recorded history, cats have lived in close contact with humans, and, since the beginning of recorded history, most humans have had strong opinions about their feline companions. Cats have been thought of as both gods and devils, as both stupid and clever, as both nasty-tempered beasts and affectionate pets. The debate over the character of cats rages on to this day.

More than 3,000 years ago, in ancient Egypt, cats were at the height of their popularity; in fact, they were considered sacred and were even worshipped. One of the most important Egyptian goddesses, Bubastis, goddess of the warmth of the sun, was drawn as having the head of a cat. One Egyptologist believes this might be for the simple reason that cats seem to like basking in sunlight so much (Antelier 14). The rulers of ancient Egypt, known as pharaohs, were also fond of cats and often kept them as treasured, pampered pets. The historian Diodorus tells us that the Egyptians thought so much of these animals that anyone who killed a cat, even accidentally, was executed (Malfi 80).

Many centuries later (but a long time ago nonetheless), in ancient Rome, cats still enjoyed a great deal of respect. They were no longer considered sacred, but they were used as a symbol of freedom and liberty, values as dear to the Romans as they are to Americans today (Vadim 127). In many statues the Roman goddess of liberty has a cat at her feet. Cat historian Strom Antelier believes that this practice stems from "the cat's refusal to be trained or restrained, for as we all know, cats come, go, and usually do just as they please" (71).

After the fall of the Roman Empire, things took a turn for the worse. The rise of Christianity during the Middle Ages caused a backlash against the beliefs of older

civilizations, such as the Egyptian, Greek, and Roman civilizations (Strickland 204). Medieval times were hard times for cats, who were considered "familiars." Familiars are the spirit slaves of witches and wizards. The belief that cats were caught up in black magic and evil possibly stems from the ancient Greek legend of Galenthias, a woman who was turned into a cat and served the goddess Hecate (Antelier 149). To the Greeks Hecate was a respectable goddess with great powers in the worlds of both the living and the dead, but by the Middle Ages, she was considered queen of the witches who performed the blackest of black magic. As if being thought of as a witch's slave were not bad enough, people in medieval times also believed that Satan himself often took the form of a black cat to walk the earth and observe unsuspecting Christians. This is why crossing paths with a black cat is considered unlucky by superstitious people even today (Antelier 157).

Cats, once protected so carefully by the Egyptians, were persecuted during this time. The Black Death, an epidemic of bubonic plague that spread from Asia to Europe and killed anywhere from one-eighth to one-third of the European population, was considered by many to be the fault of cats (Strickland 99). People gathered up as many cats as they could find and killed them mercilessly. Interestingly enough, it is now known that the plague was spread by fleas borne by rats. If people had not killed so many cats, who are good at keeping rat and mouse populations under control, perhaps they would not have had such a terrible outbreak of the disease.

Nowadays, cats are once again welcome in many homes, but whereas in ancient times all the world loved cats, today the world seems to be divided into "dog lovers" and "cat lovers." The damage done to the feline reputation during the Middle Ages has not been overcome completely. Dog lovers eye cats with suspicion and refer to them as "stupid" because cats do not like to be trained, and "stuck up" or "mean" because cats don't follow humans blindly and slobber all over their owners. Cat lovers tend to be people who admire the grace and independence of these animals, as did the ancient Romans. Of course, there are some people who like both dogs and cats, but most feel they must take sides.

Whether you think cats are gods or devils, it must be admitted that they are mysterious and intriguing creatures. Perhaps the reason they have inspired such hatred and such admiration through the years is because no one has ever been able to figure out exactly what is going on in those furry heads of theirs. It's doubtful anyone ever will.

Works Cited

Antelier, Strom. <u>Animals as Symbols: From Ancient Times to Present</u>. Pittsburgh, PA: Pennsylvania Press, 1965.

Malfi, Deirdre. <u>Whatever Pharaoh Wants, Pharaoh Gets</u>. Los Angeles, CA: Hollywood Press, 1978.

Strickland, Sandy. <u>The Dawn of the Dark Ages</u>. New York: Blue Brothers, Inc., 1984.

Vadim, Roger. <u>The Roman Pantheon</u>. New York: Political Press, 1959.

✍ EXERCISE #3 ✍
Narrowing Down Your Topic

1. Use the "Five-W and One-H" technique to narrow down this topic: Insects. Come up with at least ten questions on the topic. Pick one of those questions and then come up with five more questions based on that question.

2. Use a tree chart to narrow down this topic: Video Games. Try to make at least three main limbs and give each limb at least three branches.

3. Use a cluster chart to narrow down this topic: Deafness. Come up with at least four subtopics related to the main topic and at least two ideas per subtopic.

Choose one of the topics above that would be appropriate for a five-page report. Ask a teacher or family member if the topic you chose is a good one for a report of that length. Then begin researching the topic and write a rough draft of the five-page report. (You can even ask your teacher if you can do it for extra credit! How great would it be to get extra credit for writing about video games?) Read over the rough draft carefully and make all necessary changes and corrections. When you are done, type or rewrite the final version of the report, complete with a bibliography or works cited page.

✍ QUIZ #6 ✎
Too Broad, Too Narrow, or Just Right?

Below, sample report topics are paired with page lengths for those reports. Think about whether you could write an interesting, informative report on the given topic in the given page length. If you think the topic is too broad, write "B" in the blank. If you think it's too narrow, write "N" in the blank. If you think the topic is well balanced with the page length, write "O.K." in the blank.

____ 1. World War II—10 pages

____ 2. What makes the seasons change?—10 pages

____ 3. Building a good camp fire—15 pages

____ 4. How tadpoles turn into frogs—5 pages

____ 5. The rise and fall of communism in Russia—10 pages

____ 6. How to make a turkey sandwich—5 pages

____ 7. How to make ice—2 pages

____ 8. The Old West—10 pages

____ 9. Native American languages—15 pages

____10. The importance of buffalo to Native American tribes of the North American Great Plains—5 pages

✍ EXERCISE #4 ✎
Summary Sentences

Pretend you have to write a two-page report on each of the following topics. For each one, write a summary sentence.

1. The celebration of Halloween in America

   _____

   _____

   _____

   _____

2. Things you can do to help protect the environment

   _____

   _____

   _____

3. How dogs are used by humans

   _____

   _____

   _____

4. The most popular beaches in the United States

_____

_____

_____

5. The myth of the vampire

_____

_____

_____

Choose one of your summary sentences and write a two-page report based on it. Show the report to a teacher, family member, or friend. Ask that person to tell you which parts of the report were written well and which parts could be improved. Sometimes other people's suggestions can improve your writing.

✍ QUIZ #7 ✍
Outlining Backwards

Turn to Barnaby's report on cats on pages 112–116. Read it through and then, on a separate sheet of paper, write down what you think an outline of his report would look like.

✍ QUIZ #8 ✍
Make the Transition

The two paragraphs below are awkward and choppy. Fill the blanks with appropriate transition words or phrases to smooth them out.

1. Crazy Aunt Daisy loved to dance, and once she got going it was hard to stop her. (A) _____ she'd start swirling around like a top, her dress flying around her thighs. (B) _____ she'd begin screeching and whooping, jumping high in the air. (C) _____, all the other folks on the dance floor would start backing away, step by step, until they had their backs against the walls. Once she'd accomplished that, she'd really pull out the fancy moves. (D) _____, at my birthday party she did tumble rolls and back flips across the living room. (E) _____ a few songs, though, she'd tire out and sit down.

2. I always dreamed of traveling to Europe on a luxury ocean liner. The sea air would be invigorating. The waves would be peaceful. (A) _____, though, traveling by boat would give me the chance to develop a shipboard romance with a wealthy French businessman. Our eyes would meet across the crowded deck as we left the dock. (B) _____, just a few hours later, he would invite me to a candle-lit dinner. We would fall in love and spend every waking minute together throughout the cruise. (C) _____, just before our arrival in Europe, he would tell me he couldn't live without me and we would ask the ship's captain to marry us. (D) _____, I suppose it's possible that wealthy French businessmen might be too busy to travel by boat. Maybe I'll fly after all.

Chapter 6

The Quest "Presses" On

Captain Lucid wasted no time giving Babette, Barnaby, and Bridget their regular clothes back. Bridget was grateful to have her Yankees cap on again. Babette was also relieved—she had been most uncomfortable in her non-black outfit. Barnaby, of course, never really noticed what he was wearing.

After several military salutes and some last-minute advice on outlining, the kids were escorted to the gates, shoved outside (a little rudely they thought), and left to their own devices. . . .

As far as the eye could see, there was nothing but low, grassy prairie land. The kids had no idea what they should do, so they just sort of stood around chit-chatting.

"Well, at least we got Rule Number Two," said Bridget.

"Yeah," said Barnaby. "*Clear writing demands clear thinking*. And writing that report on cats wasn't really so hard."

"Nope," responded Bridget.

"Nice day, isn't it?" commented Barnaby, looking up at the sky.

"Yep," said Bridget, kicking at the grass.

Babette sighed and rolled her eyes. "When you two are finished discussing the weather, will you please tell me where Beauregard is?"

Barnaby and Bridget snapped to attention (maybe some of that military training had rubbed off) and began looking around. The grass and weeds were deep—waist-high in some places—so even a cat as big as Beauregard might be hard to spot. Fortunately, however, Bridget noticed a sleek black tail swishing through the weeds about twenty yards away.

"There he is!" she cried, pointing at the tail. "Is he leaving us? What is he doing?"

"Maybe he has an idea," said Barnaby, beginning to chase after the cat. "Let's go!"

"Anything is better than just standing around," agreed Babette, and she and Bridget ran off after Barnaby, whose bushy hair was now bobbing along among the foliage.

Once they caught up with Beauregard, though, he stopped, sat down, and stared expectantly at Bridget. Barnaby and Babette were rather confused, but Bridget seemed to understand.

"Guys, I think Beauregard is interested in a little air travel," she said, grinning.

I tell you what, sometimes I wonder whether those kids would remember to breathe if someone didn't remind them. There they were, in the middle of a very important quest, just lollygagging around, looking at the clouds! Hmmmph! I had to get them moving!

Of course, Bridget was the only one who could really get us moving, if you catch my drift. Since we had already reached the end of the river and there was no sign of civilization, I felt our only choice was a little hot-air ballooning, courtesy of Ms. Bridget's bubble gum. Now, as I told you before, Bridget's bubblecrafts are not without their drawbacks, but what else are you going to do when you're stuck in the middle of a prairie?

As usual, Babette and Barnaby were hesitant. Can't blame them, really. They'd had their share of misadventures on account of those bubbles. But, like I said, there was no choice. So Bridget commenced working those jaws of hers to soften up her gum. Then she waved us all back, took a deep breath, and blew and blew and blew until the enormous bubble coming out of her mouth began lifting her off the ground. Once she was about three feet up, Babette grabbed her right leg, Barnaby grabbed her left leg, and I latched onto Barnaby's lab coat. Soon we were floating through the clouds and looking at the patchwork countryside below us.

We'd learned from experience that there wasn't much you could do to steer any of Bridget's bubble vehicles. The best you could hope for was to stop them safely. And when I saw that big city and all those huge skyscrapers, and I noticed we were headed right toward it, I knew we might be in a little trouble. As we drifted closer, I began having this terrible fear that Bridget's bubble would get caught on a radio antenna or satellite dish, or that we'd just smash into a building and plummet to the ground.

I closed my eyes and gave thanks that, as a cat, I had nine lives. Then I started wondering how many of them I'd already used up. When I opened my eyes, I was hoping real hard that I had at least one left.

✎ ✎ ✎ ✎ ✎

"Bridget! Bridget! We are about to crash into that building!" yelled Babette. "Can't you do something?"

Of course, the fact that she had a hot-air balloon coming out of her mouth made it hard for Bridget to respond.

"Bridget," said Barnaby, with surprising calm. "I think I see an open window in that building about thirty feet below our current altitude. Do you think you could decrease the air pressure in the balloon to align our course with that window?"

Bridget made a questioning gesture with her hand.

"Let out some air, Bridget," he explained. "See if you can lower us. I'll tell you when to stop."

Bridget slowly sucked air out of her bubble as Barnaby talked her through it.

"Almost there . . . a little more . . . closer . . . a little more . . . no! That's too much! Pull up, I don't think we're going to clear the . . . arghhh!!"

Tumbling over the windowsill, Bridget and Babette fell flat on the desk of a grumpy-looking, gray-haired, cigar-chomping man who didn't look at all happy to see them.

He fixed them with such an angry scowl that they didn't even notice the noise from the window for a few seconds.

"Hey, help! Help!" came Barnaby's voice.

"*Rrraiirow!*" came a catlike yowl.

Babette eased herself off the desk and walked over to the window. Barnaby was hanging on to the ledge, and Beauregard seemed glued to Barnaby's leg. She grabbed hold of her friend's arms and, with a mighty yank, pulled him and the cat through the opening. After a lot of hugs and congratulations on the almost-safe landing, the questers once again noticed the man behind the desk, who sat staring at them with what seemed like barely contained rage.

"Oh, joy. Oh, happy reunion," he said through the teeth he had clenched around his cigar. "When you're done patting each other on the back, would one of you mind telling me *what you are doing in my office?*"

Bridget and Barnaby shrank back. Beauregard began to growl. Babette shushed him and turned calmly to the man.

"We are on a quest for the Lost Art of Writing," she explained. "If we do not learn all that we need to know and discover the five Rules of Good Writing, the Mute Café in Paris will be destroyed by a flood. We have learned to write letters and reports. We have learned two of the five Rules. We are now in search of our next lesson."

The man nodded, and a puff of cigar smoke circled around his head. "The Mute Café. Used to be the Muse, right? I know it well," he said, now looking more interested than mad.

Bridget and Barnaby relaxed a little and even looked hopeful.

"Well," the man continued, "you've come to the right place. And if what you say about a flood is true, we have no time to lose. My name is Dexter Fairley, but you can call me Mr. Fairley. I'm the editor of this newspaper, *The Daily Press*, which means I'm in charge. And I'm going to give you the fundamentals of journalism: **articles** and **editorials**, otherwise known as **essays.** Got your notebooks ready?"

Bridget, Babette, and Barnaby scrambled for their notebooks and borrowed some pens from Mr. Fairley.

"Good, good," said the editor. "Now, I know what you're thinking. You're thinking you're not even out of high school yet, so what do you need to learn about journalism for? *Because journalism keeps this country safe!*"

Babette and Barnaby managed to keep their faces straight, but Bridget let out a giggle.

"So, you don't believe me, eh?" snorted Fairley. "Do you know what the Bill of Rights is?"

"Sure," said Bridget, "it's the first ten amendments to the U.S. Constitution."

"Very good, kid," said Fairley. "Tell me, since you're so smart, what was the very first, most important right our founding fathers wanted to guarantee? What was amendment *numero uno*?"

"Uh, well, I . . . " stammered Bridget.

"Freedom of the press! The first amendment guarantees freedom of the press! Without free speech, without newspapers and magazines, we would fall into the black pit of ignorance! Without the open exchange of information, we would be powerless!" shrieked the editor, turning red in the face and pounding on his desk.

"Certainly is excitable, isn't he?" whispered Babette to Barnaby.

"Thomas Jefferson, our third president and the great author of the Declaration of Independence, had this to say on the matter," continued Fairley, standing up and clearing his throat loudly. "'Were it left to me to decide whether we should have a government without newspapers or newspapers without a government, I should not hesitate a moment to prefer the latter.' What a guy, huh? And a great journalist."

Fairley sat back down. "Anyway, what I'm trying to get across here is this:

- **Journalism is important.** Imagine if one person or one certain group of people controlled everything that got printed in newspapers and magazines.
  Unfortunately, that's the way things are in many countries around the world. One person or group can censor anything they don't agree with. Censorship means

changing something or cutting things out of a document altogether if they don't suit your personal purpose. Censorship is dangerous because it keeps the public from knowing what is going on around them. It keeps them from knowing the truth. Luckily, in the United States, we are guaranteed the right to publish pretty much whatever we want. Journalists—newspaper writers, magazine writers, and television and radio reporters—make it their business to keep the public informed.

- **Journalism is fun.** Most high schools and colleges publish newspapers. Some junior high schools do, too. And there are all sorts of newsletters and magazines that accept articles from young people (see pages 284–290 for a list). Some will even pay you for your work. That means you can get involved in journalism, if you're interested. You can write articles and see your name in print. You'll have fun, you'll learn all sorts of things on all sorts of topics, and you'll have the satisfaction of knowing that you are keeping your friends and classmates well informed about what's going on around them. Remember, information is power.

"So, do I make myself clear?" asked Mr. Fairley.

Bridget, Barnaby, and Babette nodded enthusiastically. Even Beauregard stayed awake for once.

"Good. Then let's begin with the factual side of things. Since you just came from Fort Report, some of this should sound familiar."

There are articles on trout fishing, articles on fashion, articles on police corruption in Brazil, articles on the bat population in Austin, Texas, and articles on the design of an atom-smashing supercollider. Magazine and newspaper articles can be written on any topic you can think of. There is one thing they all should have in common, though: facts. **All articles are factual** (with the exception of editorials and reviews, which we'll discuss later).

Newspaper and magazine articles share a common goal (to keep the public informed) and a common rule (they must stick to the facts), but structurally, they can be quite different.

NEWSPAPER ARTICLES

Think about what a newspaper is. A newspaper is a publication that, for the most part, comes out daily. It contains articles on all sorts of topics, but focuses mainly on hard news—international, national, and local events that affect people's lives. For many people, newspapers are the main source of information about what's happening in the world, and newspaper writers realize that many people are depending on them to do two things: *give it to them straight* and *give it to them fast*.

Give It to Them Straight

If people want to hear or read someone's opinion about a news story, they'll read the editorial page (we'll talk about editorials later), watch a talk show, or ask their friends what they think. What they want from newspaper articles are straight facts, and it's the reporter's duty to provide these. Here are some important guidelines reporters follow:

- **Keep your opinion to yourself.** Newspaper writers must be objective, which means that they can't let their opinions or feelings affect their articles. That can be much harder than you think. Even the best reporters can accidentally let their views seep into their writing.

- **Stick with hard facts.** Not only must reporters keep their own opinions out of their articles, they must make sure they don't treat other people's unsupported opinions as facts. Reporters must be sure their sources are reliable and honest, and often they try to confirm any information they get through other sources so they can be sure it's accurate.

- **Give all sides of the story.** Sometimes you can push your own opinion just as strongly by leaving things out of an article as you can by putting things in. To avoid giving a slanted view of something, newspaper writers must make every effort to show all sides of an issue and give all the people involved a chance to comment.

Give It to Them Fast

It would take hours to read every word of every article in a newspaper. Busy people want to read what's important to them. Headlines help them figure out which article to read, but even if they do decide to look at an article, they still might not read the whole thing. That's why the first paragraph of a newspaper article is so important.

Remember those useful question words *who, what, where, when, why,* and *how*? Well, they are six of the most important questions a reporter must answer, because the opening paragraph of any news article should pass the **Five-W, One-H Test.** That is, most, if not all, of these questions should be answered right up front—especially the first four: *who, what, where,* and *when.* The questions *why* and *how* can be answered in the body if necessary. Good newspaper articles are *not* suspenseful. Read the following paragraph, for example:

Los Angeles—Scientists taking a more thorough look at the earthquake risks posed by large faults in Southern California sharply revised their earlier predictions and said Friday there is an 86 percent chance of a very large earthquake in the region during the next 30 years.

Now put this paragraph to the test:

Who? Scientists.

What? Announced the high probability of a big earthquake.

Where? Southern California.

When? The announcement was made Friday.

The questions *why* and *how* don't really apply in this case. The rest of the article should provide background information, quotes from scientists, and reactions from local officials, all off which help flesh out the story. *The most important information is contained in the first paragraph of a newspaper article.*

Beauregard says sports and entertainment are different. The rules and guidelines of newspaper writing don't apply to *every* section of a newspaper. For instance, sports writers have a style all their own. They want their coverage of game to be exciting they want to make readers feel like they were there—so sports writers don't always answer questions like *where* and *when* in the first paragraph. Entertainment and travel writers *must* include opinions in their writing because the enjoyment of books, movies, music, and travel are matters of personal taste. Think about the purpose of the sports section or entertainment section, then think about the purpose of the national and local news sections, and you'll understand why this is the case.

One way reporters save time and space is by using **newspaper style.** Newspaper writers aren't very concerned with making their writing graceful, beautiful, entertaining, or snappy. They may not even care if their writing is considered dry or choppy. They want to get the facts across as clearly and quickly as possible.

Here are the elements of basic newspaper style:

Use simple, basic sentences. Subject-verb-object is the arrangement of most sentences in a newspaper article. For example, "Mayor Donovan announced deep budget cuts in the city police department, effective from January" or "Firefighters rescued two children from a burning house." You wouldn't write "As their home and precious belongings burned to ashes around them, two innocent children were snatched from the jaws of death and brought to safety by fearless heroes from the local fire department." It may be more exciting, but it takes three times as long to read (and write).

Cut unnecessary adjectives, adverbs, and descriptions. Don't include anything that isn't directly related to your story. Take this sentence, for example: "Firefighters rescued two innocent, blond children from a burning house." It doesn't really matter that the children were innocent or blond, does it? Those words should be cut.

Here's another example: "Wearing a wrinkled and ill-fitting floral print dress, Mrs. Duffy, her grief-stricken, pale face swollen from crying, wearily took the stand Wednesday to testify against Horace Humphrey, the long-haired, well-mannered Greenville man accused of murdering her husband, the late Mr. Duffy."

Most of that sentence is unnecessary. What Mrs. Duffy wore, how her face looked, or what the accused murderer looked like are unimportant. The sentence should read: "Mrs. Duffy took the stand Wednesday to testify against Horace Humphrey, the man accused of murdering her husband."

Don't worry about transitions (not *too* much, anyway). When you're writing a school report or paper, it's important for your writing to be smooth and polished. But in a newspaper article, quick and clear are the most important qualities. Use transition words only if leaving them out would make your meaning unclear.

Writing a Newspaper Article

Getting ready to write a newspaper article is a lot like getting ready to write a research paper. First you have to do research. Then you write a summary sentence and an outline. Then you write your piece. Your sources of information and your style, however, are completely different. Read through the following steps.

STEP 1: Gather information

When you work for a newspaper, either your editor assigns you a story or you hear about something interesting and pursue it yourself. There's no one way to go about getting information, but some of the standard tactics include asking the people involved for information, contacting experts on the subject, and monitoring a situation firsthand (this is **investigative journalism**).

Say the editor of your school paper told you there was a rumor that the "hamburgers" served in the school cafeteria weren't really made of meat but of a soy-based substitute. You could ask the head cook at the cafeteria for a comment. You could talk to the principal. You could go into the kitchen and see where they store the "hamburger" patties, and see whether there's some kind of labeling. You could take a sample of one of the burgers to your science teacher and ask her if there's any way to figure out whether it's meat or soy. Keep digging until you have the whole story. If the burgers are made of soy, why aren't they called soy burgers? Were the burgers sold in the cafeteria ever made of meat? If so, why did the school decide to switch? What do students think about the soy burgers?

STEP 2: Write your "lead"

"Lead" is a journalistic term for the essence of a story—the most important thing. Good articles must open with a strong lead that quickly lays out the most vital facts. Bad articles "bury the lead," which means they don't get to the good stuff until later in the article, or they miss the point entirely.

A lead is pretty much the same thing as a *summary sentence* (see pages 85–86). To figure out what your lead should be, ask yourself why people would care about the information you have gathered. What would they care about most? What would affect their behavior or their lives? In our story about the soy burgers, the lead for an article in the school paper could be "'Switching from pure meat hamburgers to soy burgers two years ago has saved Goodwyn Junior High School a total of $15,550,' Principal B. F. Nicker said in an interview last Friday." But your classmates probably don't care about how much money the school saved. A better lead would be "Principal B. F. Nicker and a cafeteria cook confirmed reports Friday that in October 2002, the Goodwyn Junior High School lunchroom began serving soy-based patties instead of meat patties in their hamburgers without notifying students of this substitution or changing the price of the burgers."

STEP 3: Write your outline

Even if your article is going to be short, it's a good idea to jot down an outline. It always helps to think things through before you start. See pages 87–89 for an explanation of how to write an outline.

In a newspaper article, your introduction is your lead. The body is background information, comments and information from the people involved, and reactions from people affected by a given situation. You don't have to worry about a conclusion. Once you've given all the information you have, you're done.

STEP 4: Write your article

Remember to use the simple, direct newspaper style. Break your writing into paragraphs frequently—this makes it easier to read.

STEP 5: Check it over

Check your grammar and spelling, and make sure your article is easy to understand. Did you present all sides of the issue or event? Did you give a fair and balanced picture of what happened? Did you check your sources? Did you keep your opinions to yourself? If everything checks out, you're done. Turn in your article.

Beauregard says reporters can change the course of history. Newspaper writers have the power to uncover injustices and abuses in our society. Many crimes and wrongs have first been brought to light by newspapers. Some famous journalists and their accomplishments are

Nellie Bly—A reporter for *The New York World* in the early 1900s who uncovered the terrible conditions and abuses in mental institutions. Her real name was Elizabeth Seaman.

Bob Woodward and Carl Bernstein—Two reporters for the *Washington Post* who uncovered the truth behind a break-in at the Watergate office building in 1972 by men working for President Richard Nixon. Nixon was forced to resign the presidency because of the scandal surrounding the crime.

Charles Edward Russell—Exposed filthy conditions in turn-of-the-century meatpacking plants that eventually led to federal laws on meat inspection.

✎ ✎ ✎ ✎ ✎

"I am so excited!" gasped Babette. "I cannot wait to begin writing journalistic articles!"

"Well, too bad," said Mr. Fairley, quite simply.

"What do you mean? You have just shown us the way to write good articles!" she replied, somewhat hurt.

"Sure, you know all the steps, but you don't know the most important Rule, the one that applies to newspaper writers, magazines writers—heck, writers of every kind."

"Rule?" said Bridget. "Did he say Rule?"

"He sure did," said Barnaby, his pen poised and ready.

"So you have the first two Rules," continued Fairley. "And here is the third Rule. . . ."

RULE #3
Know your audience.

"Know your audience?" puzzled Bridget. "What does that mean? We can't actually go out and meet the people who would read our articles."

"Maybe not," replied Fairley, "but in order to write something they'll enjoy, you have to know a little something about them. Take that example I gave about soy burgers in the school cafeteria. If you were writing that article for a newsletter that is mainly read by school superintendents, you would probably focus on the cost savings involved in switching from meat to soy. But for students, the important thing is taste. Before you begin writing, you must know what makes your audience tick."

"Ah, I think I understand what you mean," replied Barnaby. "For instance, newspaper articles are written for the general public. The general public cares about the quality of life in their country, their health, their safety, and the health and safety of their families. Beyond that, I can't really say much about them for sure. But if I were writing an article for a scientific journal, I could assume a lot about my audience. They probably have a good background in science and a sharp interest in scientific research and discoveries."

"Precisely, my boy," said Fairley. "Actually, you have brought us to our next topic, which is writing magazine articles."

MAGAZINE ARTICLES

Magazine articles differ from newspaper articles in a number of ways. Feature articles in magazines are usually longer than the average newspaper article. They can involve deeper research and preparation. Plus, the strict newspaper style doesn't apply to magazine articles. In magazines, you can get a little fancier with your writing. You don't have to worry about cramming all the most important details into the lead. You can be more creative with your introductions and conclusions. One thing remains the same, though: Magazine articles must be factual and objective.

The steps for writing a magazine article are the same as for writing a newspaper article (see the steps on pages 137–140), but there are some special considerations.

Tone, Focus, and Audience

There are all sorts of magazines out there designed for pretty much any group of people who share common interests. There are magazines for freshwater fishers, magazines for teenage girls, magazines for teenage boys, magazines for middle-aged women, magazines for fashion-conscious men, magazines for truckers, magazines for coin collectors, magazines for dog lovers—magazines for everybody!

Obviously, the readers of these magazines have different amounts of knowledge. Your readers determine the **tone** and **focus** of your article. Tone is the overall style of the article—lighthearted, serious, formal, casual, or whatever. Focus is what part of a story or topic you decide to pay attention to.

For example, say you were writing an article on a new kind of surgery that corrects nearsightedness so people don't have to wear glasses. If you were writing that article for a general interest magazine such as *Time,* you couldn't assume your readers know very much about how the eye works or about surgery. They would be interested mainly in how the surgery could help *them.* That would be your focus. You would tell the reader how much the procedure costs and what the advantages and disadvantages are. You would give a basic explanation of the surgery. The tone of the article might be upbeat, like "Hey, everyone, isn't science wonderful?"

If you were writing the article for the *Journal of the American Medical Association,* your readers would all be doctors who know a whole bunch about how the eye works. They would want a detailed description of the surgery and the equipment required. They would want to know about tests on the safety and long-term effects of the procedure. The tone would probably be very serious and straightforward.

Get the idea? If not, try gathering up whatever magazines you have around the house. Look at the pictures in them. Read a couple of the articles. How would you describe the writing and the general "feel" of the magazine? Can you picture what a reader of that magazine might be like? (You should be able to—if the magazine is in your house, someone in your family reads it.)

 **Beauregard says** the freelance life is a cool job option. When you get out of school, you'll have to get a job (unless you marry into royalty or win the lottery). How about a career in which you could wear whatever you want while working, sleep in late when you want, and devote your time to whatever interests you most? That's what being a freelance writer is like. "Freelance" means you work for yourself, not for one company. Freelance writers write articles on any topic that interests them—anything from traveling through Australia to auto racing to the latest designer clothing collections in Italy. Then they sell these articles to magazines.

Of course, someone has to want to *read* these articles. That's why most freelance writers talk about their ideas with the editors of magazines they think might publish them *before* they start writing.

✎ ✎ ✎ ✎ ✎

"It sounds like learning to write well can help you a lot," said Bridget. "You can even make a living at it."

"Being a writer can be just as important as being a doctor, a police officer, or a politician," added Barnaby.

"That's true," agreed Fairley. "Important and fun—that's what I said from the beginning. But so far, we've only paid attention to the facts. Journalists have an obligation to uphold the truth and keep their opinions to themselves. But *some* writers get paid to give their opinions. People read their stuff because they want to know what these people have to say."

"But I thought all articles were factual," said Babette.

"These are different. These pieces are **editorials** or **reviews.** The people who write editorials are called either **editorialists** or **columnists,** and the people who write reviews are called **critics.**"

EDITORIALS AND COLUMNS

Every newspaper has an editorial section in which staff writers or freelance writers publish **editorials.** Editorials often express strong opinions about current events. They can offer ideas about and explanations of what's going on in the news. Editorials are important counterparts to news stories because certain issues can be very complicated. Interpretations and explanations are pretty much the same thing as opinions (the same set of facts can be looked at many ways), so news writers steer clear of drawing too many conclusions. That's where editorials come in.

One example is presidential election campaigns. Each person who runs for president has something called a "platform," which is a set of issues that the candidate thinks are important and a plan of what the candidate would do if elected. Say for example that part of Candidate X's platform is that the United States should be the first country to put a person on Mars. News writers can report only what Candidate X has to say on that topic and what Candidates Y and Z say. But editorialists can say the idea is "irresponsible" if they want. They can point out that putting a person on Mars would cost millions and millions of dollars and that the money would be better spent curing fatal diseases. Or, on the other hand, they could praise Candidate X for having a pioneering spirit.

Editorialists often write a regular **column** for their newspapers. Some editorial columns are **syndicated,** which means that several newspapers or magazine "subscribe" to that column and pay a fee to publish it.

Newspapers and magazines also accept editorials from outside sources. People who feel strongly about a subject can contribute their articles.

Writing an Editorial

Writing an editorial is a matter of personal style. Read some of the editorials in your newspaper and you'll see they all have different ways of getting their points across. Some use humor, some use sarcasm, and some use personal stories and anecdotes.

If you want to write an editorial, follow these guidelines.

STEP 1: Write a summary sentence

Yep, it's summary sentence time again. Why do we keep suggesting that you write these things? Let's refer to Rule 2: *Clear writing demands clear thinking.* Writing summary sentences is a good way to make sure you've thought through your ideas and have a clear plan for your writing.

STEP 2: Write an outline

Feel like you've heard this one before too? Good. Writing an outline gives you a handy road map so you won't get lost or lose direction when you write.

STEP 3: Support your opinion with specifics

As you write your editorial, try to use examples to prove each point. Be specific and you will be much more convincing.

STEP 4: Check it over

Before sending anything off or handing anything in, it's always a good idea to read it over for mistakes.

REVIEWS

One of the most loved, hated, feared, and respected writers is the critic, the person who writes reviews. Reviews are articles that praise good points and criticize bad points of books, plays, movies, music, art, operas, ballets, and restaurants, and whether any of these things receives a good or bad review can determine its success or failure. People rely on reviews to help them make up their minds about what movies to see, where to eat, and what books to buy.

What qualifies a person to be a critic? Well, a lot of unhappy authors, actors, and chefs will tell you that anyone with an opinion and a typewriter can be a critic, and they'd be partly right. To be a *good* critic, though, you must have a strong background in the area you cover.

For example, to be a movie critic, it helps if you are familiar with all the different parts of moviemaking— lighting, set design, editing, directing, sound, cinematography, and so on. It also helps if you have studied filmmaking and watched many, many movies. That way, to put it bluntly, you will know what you're talking about.

Most high school and college newspapers carry reviews. Being a critic for a newspaper can be great fun (especially as you often get free passes to movies, free books, or free CDs from people who want you to write about their work). Pick the area you are most interested in and learn as much as you can about it.

If you are into music, for instance, listen to as many different kinds of music as you can lay your hands on. Go to the library and check out books on the history of music. If you don't play an instrument, learn a little about music theory and how songs are put together. Learn about sound engineering. Learn about the music industry itself. Sound like a lot of work? Well, you don't have to do it all at once. But you'll be surprised—the more you know about music (or books, or art, or movies), the more you'll appreciate it.

As far as the actual writing of a review goes, follow the same steps as you would for an editorial. And remember, specifics are important. If you just say, "Bonehead's new song, 'Pothole,' really stinks," it won't be as convincing as saying, "Bonehead's new song, 'Pothole,' has a lifeless beat and boring two-chord structure made even more annoying by the lead singer's whining chorus, 'I am a pothole, baby, I'll pop your tire.'"

WHAT ABOUT ESSAYS?

Essays are short literary pieces on one topic, and they usually include the author's opinion. Sounds like an editorial, doesn't it? Essays and editorials are almost exactly the same, except newspapers and magazines don't publish essays very often anymore.

Not that essays aren't interesting; it's just that they don't necessarily deal with current events or everyday matters. Essay writing has a noble history stretching back to ancient Greece and Rome, where philosophers wrote essays on the nature of reality and existence. In fact, "the human condition" has been a popular theme for essay-writing philosophers for thousands of years. René Descartes, Michel de Montaigne, Immanuel Kant, and David Hume, among others, all wrote famous essays on the subject.

More recently (that is, a couple hundred years ago), a more popular topic was government. Thomas Paine, John Stuart Mill, Adam Smith, Henry David Thoreau, and John Locke wrote essays that directly affected the history of this country and others. The essays of Thoreau, for example, influenced both Mahatma Gandhi, a leader in the movement for Indian independence, and Dr. Martin Luther King, Jr., our country's most famous civil rights leader.

But not all essays have to be on "big" issues like existence or politics. Jorge Luis Borges, an Argentinian author, wrote an essay on blindness. A. Whitney Brown (who used to appear on the television show *Saturday Night Live*) wrote an essay called "How Maple Syrup Elects Our Presidents." You could write an essay on the joys of Ping-Pong, if you wanted. You could reflect in essay form on the dream-lives of cats. You could wonder who invented shoelaces, and why. Anything you think about, wonder about, or have an opinion on could be the subject of an essay.

If you want to write an essay, follow the same steps as you would for an editorial (see pages 148–149).

Beauregard says essays still count. Even though people don't read as many essays as they used to, essay writing is not dead. When it comes to applying to college, essay writing is still alive and kicking. Most competitive schools will require that you write at least one essay on a topic they give you, so it might be in your best interest to try it out. There are also essay-writing contests you could enter.

✎ ✎ ✎ ✎ ✎

"So, are you kids ready to start your careers as journalists?" asked Fairley. His cigar had burned down almost to his lips.

Barnaby, Bridget, and Babette nodded enthusiastically.

"Good, good, but I'm afraid I'm going to have to kick you out now," he said. "You're on a quest, remember? And unless I miss my guess, you're only halfway through with it."

The questers shook their heads in disbelief.

"Halfway? You can't be serious," groaned Bridget.

"Oh, I'm always serious. See, you've only learned about nonfiction writing so far. Now it's time to explore your more creative side. But first, before I turn you loose, let's see if you caught the gist of what I was telling you. Try the following exercises.

✍ EXERCISE #5 ✍
Rewrite the Lead

Below are five flawed opening lines for news articles. Figure out what is wrong with them, and then rewrite the lead in correct newspaper style. Hint: Get rid of all the descriptive words and phrases that would have nothing to do with a news story.

1. Just in time, Officer McKay arrived at the scene to apprehend the three jewel thieves and their pet dog Alonzo.

2. The Secretary of State, a bald man with dimples wearing a rumpled Brooks Brothers suit, flew to Tibet today for an important round of trade talks.

3. Ms. Lentil, who had five fingers on each hand and five toes on each foot, was awarded the Klostovik medal of honor.

4. After two layovers, three mediocre in-flight meals, and a stretch of turbulence that made one of the flight attendants puke, the governor arrived safely in Boston after leaving California.

✍ EXERCISE #6 ✍
Write a Newspaper Article

Write an article about something that is going on at your school. If your school has a newspaper, try to get the article published in the next issue. You can write about any current event that is related to your school—changes in the cafeteria menu, renovations to the school, an issue related to the neighborhood where your school is located, the outcome of a game or competition that a school team participated in, the hiring of a new principal or teacher, a bake sale to raise money, etc. You get the idea. Now, go out and find that story!

Chapter 7

Observations from On High

DIARIES, JOURNALS, NOTEBOOKS

I tell you what, after all Mr. Fairley's talk about being a reporter, I was ready to go out and start a whole new career! Not that I've actually had a career, mind you. I've been a spy for the Elephant Empire, a first mate on a merchant marine freighter, a movie projectionist, a Balinese sword-swallower, an actuary—ah, so many different things. But this idea of writing for a living sounded great!

   Unfortunately, whatever plans I may have had were put on hold. Fairley insisted we continue the Quest for the Lost Art of Writing immediately. He was so insistent that we get out of his office, in fact, I half expected him to throw us out the window we came in through. Luckily, he allowed us go out in the hall and wait for the elevator.

Bridget, Babette, and Barnaby weren't talking much. I guess they were still trying to let what they had learned sink in. So when the elevator came, we all just got in and stood there quietly, the way people in elevators normally do. Pretty soon, though, Bridget broke the silence.

✎ ✎ ✎ ✎ ✎

"Hey," said Bridget, "I think we're going up instead of down. Did one of you push the wrong button or something?"

"I didn't push anything," shrugged Barnaby.

"I did not push anything either," said Babette.

"Oh, well," sighed Bridget. "I guess we'll just head back down once we reach the top."

The office building they were in was very tall, and it took quite some time for them to get all the way up. When the elevator doors finally opened, the questers found themselves on the roof. The building was by far the tallest in the whole city, and the view from up there was breathtaking, but what attracted their attention most was the fact that a small airplane was parked about twenty feet in front of them.

The airplane looked pretty old: It had a propeller on the front and double wings with huge eyes painted on them like some sort of insignia. It wasn't closed up like modern planes are, either. In front of the airplane was a tall, thin woman dressed in a brown leather bomber jacket and an aviator cap with goggles. She was busy fixing the propeller and seemed not to notice the approach of Barnaby, Babette, Bridget, and Beauregard. But when they were almost near enough to get a good look at her, she spoke.

"Say, do one of you kids happen to have a wrench?" she said, without even looking up.

Barnaby jumped back, a little startled. "What? I . . . um, I mean who?"

The pilot turned and smiled at him. Shiny red curls squeezed out of the bottom of her aviator cap, and even with her big goggles on, he could see she had a sprinkling of freckles across her nose.

"You, that's who," she said with a laugh. "Got a wrench?"

Barnaby began scratching his bushy head of hair with a sort of frown on his face. Bridget nudged Babette with her elbow. Whenever Barnaby scratched his head, something interesting fell out—interesting, though not always useful. This time, however, a large shiny wrench came clattering to the ground at his feet.

"I *thought* I had a wrench up there," he said with a blush. The pilot was smiling broadly at him as he offered her the tool. After making a couple of quick adjustments, she stood back and looked at the propeller with satisfaction.

"There," she said. "That ought to do it. Thanks, kid."

She tossed the wrench back to Barnaby and wiped her hands on her snug tan pants.

"I'm Athena Airborne," she said, stretching out her hand to shake with Barnaby, "but you can call me Peeper. Most everybody does."

"Pleased to meet you, Peeper. My name's Barnaby, and these are my friends Babette, Bridget, and Beauregard," he replied politely.

Hands and paws were shaken all around. After that, there was an awkward pause in the conversation as Peeper looked them up and down, pulled a little notepad out of her pocket, and scribbled something down.

"So," she started, pen still in hand. "What are you all up to? I mean, what brings you to this roof?"

"We could ask you the same thing, Ms., uh, Peeper," snapped Bridget suspiciously. "Landing planes on a roof isn't what you'd call usual."

A corner of Peeper's mouth curled up into a smile. "No, I suppose not," she said. "But I was having trouble with my propeller. And you . . . ?"

Bridget clamped her mouth shut and folded her arms over her chest. She wasn't too fond of nosy people. Babette, on the other hand, saw no reason not to answer. Actually, she kind of liked explaining their mission to people.

"We are on a Quest for the Lost Art of Writing," she proclaimed, trying not to sound too impressed with herself. "So far we have learned many things, but we have not yet discovered the secrets of fiction—writing that comes from our hearts and imaginations. If we do not succeed in our quest, the Mute Café in Paris will be washed away by a flood. The water was rising when we left."

Peeper nodded and scribbled a few more notes to herself. "It's a lucky thing I found you," she said solemnly. "I used to go to the Muse—that's what it used to be called—whenever I was in Paris. I'll do whatever possible to save it."

"You mean you can help us?" gasped Barnaby. He had not thought this redheaded pilot would be much of a writing fan.

"Sure," she said. "Tell you what: Why don't you kids climb into the plane? You too, Beauregard. Let's slip these surly bonds of Earth—I think better in the air!"

The questers wasted no time scrambling aboard. Peeper adjusted her goggles and handed each of her passengers a pair. It took some fixing to get the goggles to stay on Beauregard's head without pulling his fur, but they managed. Once Peeper got the propeller spinning, it was only a few more seconds before they were soaring noisily toward the clouds.

After a while, Peeper leveled off the airplane and began to speak.

"You see these eyes on my wings?" she asked. "They are my trademark, my own personal sign. Eyes are for looking, for observing. That's why they call me Peeper—because I always keep my peepers peeled."

Bridget and Barnaby giggled. Babette just blinked, probably because she didn't know that "peepers" are eyes. But their pilot just kept right on talking.

"A good writer notices things and thinks about them," she continued. "She notices not just with her eyes, but with her ears and nose and hands—with everything! Most people just bumble through life not paying any attention to what's going on around them. They don't notice that fresh mowed grass smells bitter and comforting at the same time. They don't notice that the first drop of rain in a summer shower feels like a kiss when it hits your skin. They don't notice how cream swirls like storm clouds when you pour it into hot coffee. They don't remember the exact day they met their best friend, or what they said, or how they felt. But good writers notice and remember."

Bridget, Babette, and Barnaby frowned, thinking about all the things they might have overlooked or forgotten.

"What are we supposed to do?" asked Babette. "We cannot remember everything. How do we know what is important?"

"What is important is completely up to you," answered Peeper. "But you won't know what is important to you if you don't know how to *observe*. Here are a few techniques.

- **Open yourself to your surroundings.** You have five senses: sight, hearing, smell, taste, and touch. Use them. Notice how different places smell different—your school, your home, the doctor's office. Notice how it feels to step into a bathtub full of water. Notice the taste of an orange popsicle. Notice how your hair feels after you wash it. Notice what color the sky is right before the sun disappears. Just notice what's around you. You'd be surprised at the number of interesting things you miss every day just because you don't take the time to listen or touch or smell.

- **Keep your mouth shut.** Stop yammering and listen to what other people are saying and how they are saying it. Notice what they are doing. Try to keep yourself apart from what's going on and just look and listen as if you were at a movie. (Don't do this all the time, of course. Only when you feel like observing.) You'll notice all sorts of weird things—like maybe your brother finishes every sentence with the words "you know?" Or your mother fidgets with her earrings when she's nervous. Maybe one of your classmates sighs and stares whenever you walk by. But you can't see or hear any of this if you're too busy talking.

- **Plot a new course.** A lot of the time, people don't notice their surroundings because they are so used to them. They get into ruts—like sitting in the same seat on the school bus every day, or eating the same thing for lunch, or always walking the same route from place to place. You can get a whole new look at your world and jump-start your observation skills by making a few small changes. Sit in a different seat in the cafeteria at lunch. Talk to someone you don't usually talk to. Go in a different entrance than you usually do at school. It doesn't seem like a big deal, but small changes can change your perspective (that means point of view) in a big way and help you see things you never thought were there.

❧ ❧ ❧ ❧ ❧

"I guess that's why I like flying so much," continued Peeper. "It helps me change my perspective. Just look at the ground below us. The patches of farmland, the river. Feel how cool the air is up here."

Barnaby, Babette, Bridget, and Beauregard all busied themselves observing their surroundings.

"Now, then," said Peeper. "Let's see if you have the hang of this. Before we go on, I have to know if your senses are in working order. Try these exercises.

✍ EXERCISE #7 ✍
The Five Senses

For each of the following, pretend you are trying to explain what you see, hear, smell, taste, or feel to someone who has never experienced what you are describing. Don't just use words like *bad* or *good* or *nice*—really try to explain.

1. Sight: Describe the look of your classroom in detail. What kind of chairs are there? Exactly what is on the walls? What does your teacher's desk look like? How many windows are there? What can you see outside the windows? What kind of floor—tile? wood? Write down everything you can *see*— at least two paragraphs.

2. Hearing: Describe in words the following sounds: The sound you hear when you press your hands hard against your ears; the sound of your doorbell; the sound of someone scratching his fingernails across a chalkboard; the sounds you hear during lunchtime in a crowded cafeteria. Write a few sentences describing each sound.

3. Smell: Describe the following smells: The smell of a full bag of garbage; what you smell when you hug your mother or father; the smell of the gym at school; the smell of the

soap you use in your bath. Write a few sentences describing each smell.

4. Taste: Describe the following tastes: A spoonful of fruit punch mix; unsweetened iced tea; buttered toast; strawberries. Write a few sentences describing each taste.

5. Touch: Describe how the following things feel: Walking barefoot on the pavement in summer; jumping into a pool of cool water; petting a cat or a dog; getting into bed when it's cold outside. Write a few sentences describing each of these things.

✎ ✎ ✎ ✎ ✎

"Are all systems go?" asked Peeper.

"Yep," said Bridget. Babette and Barnaby nodded.

"Okay, let's talk about a kind of writing many writers do, and that is **keeping a journal.** A journal can be different things to different people. A journal can be a fancy hardback book with nice paper, or a regular spiral notebook, or a file on your computer, or a bunch of scrap paper. The great thing about journals is, there are no rules. In a journal, *you can write whatever you want.* The following are some reasons people keep journals.

- **It's fun to look back.** Many people keep journals or diaries to record their feelings and thoughts and the events of their everyday lives so they can hold on to them better. Imagine keeping a diary now, then ten years from now looking back on what you wrote. Chances are you will have changed a lot, and you might enjoy looking back at the person you were. It's kind of like a personal growth chart.

- **Keep track of ideas.** As you start observing more and more, ideas for writing will come to you. Many writers like to keep a notebook with them to write down these ideas and observations whenever they come. Sometimes they write down pieces of conversation they hear, or interesting phrases. They might use these in stories or poems later.

- **Express difficult or special feelings.** Writing in a journal is a good way to work out feelings like sadness, anger, confusion, or frustration, especially when you have a hard time talking about these feelings with other people. It's also a good way to explore joy or love. Sometimes people sort of talk to themselves when they write in their journals. Sometimes they talk to the people who are causing their feelings—like writing a letter to someone without sending it. Very often, writing about your feelings can help you understand them better, which helps you deal with them better.

Beauregard says journals can be literary, too. Many writers and other famous people have kept diaries and journals. Some of these diaries were published, and they became very important pieces of literature. For example, many of you may have heard of *The Diary of Anne Frank*. Anne Frank was a young Jewish girl who kept a diary while hiding from the Nazis during World War II; this diary has been read by millions of people in countries all around the world. Ask your librarian to help you find published diaries of interesting people.

Samples from an Observation Notebook

When I watched the people diving into the swimming pool, I thought about the water's ability to completely touch them. Air and water can touch a person totally. I was jealous of that ability.

Sitting on the bus today, conversation behind me:

Girl #1: "What time is it?"
Girl #2: "Do you mean now?"

Mr. Gleason looks like a lizard when he
laughs. Eyes bulge out and throat jiggles.
Almost expect him to stick out a forked
tongue. Lizard laugher. Lizard laughter.
Some people you just shouldn't tell jokes to.

The stone bench under the tree is cool and
smooth and smells like moss. I like it, but it
kind of reminds me of a tombstone. Do I like
it because it reminds me of a tombstone?

✎ ✎ ✎ ✎ ✎

"If you're not in the habit, keeping a diary or
journal may take a little getting used to," said
Peeper. "There are a couple of things you can
do to make it easier, though. First, if you want
to keep a diary of events in your life, set aside a
certain time each day for writing. Maybe right
before you go to bed or when you come home
from school. Once you get into the routine,
you'll find yourself looking forward to writing.

"If you're interested in writing down ideas
and observations, keep a small notebook and
pen with you at all times. You can find small
notepads that will easily fit in your pocket. As
soon as an idea pops into your head, whip out
that notebook and write it down! You might
not have time to flesh it out completely,

especially if you're in the middle of class, but write what you can. Then, when you have time, expand on the ideas you like."

"But what if I want to keep a diary *and* write down observations?" asked Bridget. "Do I have to keep them separate?"

The pilot laughed. "No, of course not! Your journal is your personal writing place. Many people have journals that are filled with diary entries, random thoughts, song lyrics, pieces of poems, half-finished stories—whatever they want!"

"I'm not sure I understand all this," sighed Bridget. "I want to learn to write a journal the *right* way."

"There is no right way," said Peeper patiently. "Journals can be many things, as I said. One of the most important things they do is help build your writing skills and loosen up your imagination. Think of your writing skills as a set of muscles in your body. The more you exercise them, the stronger they become. And journals are great exercise."

"Are there other things we can do to strengthen our writing skills and imaginations?" asked Babette.

"I'm glad you asked that, kid," said Peeper. "Here are a couple of variations on the standard journal.

Clip files—Writers often find inspiration in other writers. You might find an article in a magazine or newspaper that interests you. You might find a poem or part of a story you like. Photocopy it and keep it in a special file. When you do this, try to figure out what it is you like about the piece. Maybe it's just the subject matter—for instance, maybe it's an article on bats, and you think bats are cool. But maybe it's something about the writing itself you like—the way the author keeps the action going in a story or the way something is described in a poem.

Dream logs—Keeping a dream log, which is a record of your dreams, is a truly weird experience, but many great ideas can come out of it. Dream logs are especially useful for people who don't think they are very creative. Maybe you don't have a wild imagination while you're awake, but you might while you're asleep!

If you're like most people, you can remember some of your dreams clearly when you first wake up, but they fade throughout the day. To keep a dream log, then, you should keep a notepad and pen right next to your bed. As soon as you wake up, before you even get out of bed, grab that notebook and write down everything you can remember: thoughts, fears, feelings, descriptions. Don't worry about grammar and spelling and making sense, just write everything down as quickly as you can.

Beauregard says get surreal. Many artists and writers rely heavily on their dreams for inspiration, especially a group of twentieth-century writers and artists known as *surrealists*. Something that is surreal is dreamlike or not realistic. Salvador Dali and René Magritte are good examples of surrealist painters (you can find examples of their paintings in books on modern art). Science fiction, fantasy, and horror writers also draw on their dreams for ideas.

✎ ✎ ✎ ✎ ✎

"Hey," said Bridget. "Are we going down?"

"How *observant* of you," giggled Babette.

"Yes, in fact, I've told you everything I can," said Peeper. "Hopefully, I've opened your eyes. Reach under your seats. There should be four parachutes."

"Parachutes? You mean, you're not going to land?" gulped Barnaby, a little panicked.

"Nope. But don't worry, I've pulled below the cloud cover. It should be an easy jump. Just count to ten and pull the cord on the vest. Simple."

"Take it easy, Barnaby," Bridget said comfortingly, pulling the parachutes out. "It's not like you're a stranger to heights."

Barnaby sighed and grumbled and reluctantly took the parachute she handed him. Babette and Bridget strapped a parachute on Beauregard, and they sat in uneasy silence for a second before Bridget asked, "Are we just supposed to climb out?"

"Oh," said Peeper. "This part's easy."

And with that she pulled back on her controls and sent the plane into a dramatic barrel roll that turned the aircraft upside down and shook the questers out of their seats and into mid-air.

"Ahhhhhhhhhhhh! " they yelled as they tumbled through the open space.

"Good luck!" yelled Peeper as she flew out of sight. "And don't forget to pull those cords!"

Chapter 8

Peaceful Thoughts by the Plum Trees

POETRY

I yanked that parachute cord with my teeth and hoped for the best. To tell the truth, I was more worried about Bridget, Barnaby, and Babette than myself. Cats, you see, can fall from great heights without hurting themselves. In fact, that's why I was such a popular trapeze artist back when I was traveling with the Vladvostok and O'Malley Circus in the Ukraine. I could do my act without a net and not really worry about it. I wowed audiences in every village from Odessa to Minsk!

But anyway, after the initial scare of being dumped out of an airplane wore off, I think we all quite enjoyed our skydiving . . . at least for a while. It was several minutes before we noticed that we were over an ocean, and I don't think I have to tell you that I was not pleased at the idea of getting wet. Luckily, however, there appeared to be a few small islands dotting the water. We did our best to steer ourselves toward the one with the most open space so we wouldn't get hung up on some trees. Unfortunately, once you pull that cord and release your chute, it's almost impossible to steer yourself.

✎ ✎ ✎ ✎ ✎

"Man, oh man!" yelled Bridget.

"Yaaarrgh!" screeched Barnaby.

"Eeeeeeoooiiiii!" wailed Babette.

The questers were falling right toward a bunch of strange-looking trees, and even with their parachutes up, their descent was much faster than they were comfortable with. But since there was nothing they could do about it, they just closed their eyes and crossed their fingers.

They all let out a big "Ummmph!" as they felt their falls abruptly stopped before they hit the ground. On opening their eyes, they discovered that they were about ten feet off the ground dangling from the branches of a gnarly old tree. Looking up at them was an old man with white hair, a thin white beard, and smooth, almost youthful Asian features. He wore a beautiful, sky-blue silk robe with fancy silver embroidery around the edges. Even though he wasn't exactly smiling, he was obviously amused at the awkward situation in which Barnaby, Babette, Bridget, and Beauregard found themselves. He spoke to them:

"I have visitors, Snowflakes unmuddied by earth: A gift from the sky."

"He sure does talk strangely," grumbled Bridget, wriggling in her parachute vest.

"Yes, he does," mused Barnaby. "Excuse me, sir. Pardon us for, er, dropping in on you like this, but do you think you could help us down?"

The man nodded and ran off through the trees.

"Hey, wait! Come back!" yelled Barnaby.

"I think he will return," said Babette calmly. And sure enough, the man was back a couple of minutes later with a ladder and a knife. One by one, he stationed the ladder under them, cut them down, and helped them to the ground.

Babette, after straightening her hair and tucking in her shirt, introduced everyone and explained that they were on a quest for the Lost Art of Writing. The man considered them, his dark eyes twinkling, for a few seconds before replying, "I am Ikiko. I believe I can help you. You will come with me."

With that, he turned and began walking back through the trees. It was all Bridget, Babette, and Barnaby could do to keep up with the nimble old man (Beauregard had no trouble, being a cat and naturally agile). The kids kept tripping over roots and stumps, but the old man never slowed down or turned to see if they were still following. Finally, after the children were almost out of breath, they came to a clearing and saw a temple with a roof that turned up at the ends. The columns supporting the roof were ornately carved. Beside the temple was a little stream shining with red and yellow fish. And all around them were plum trees, blooming sweetly.

"This is absolutely beautiful," sighed Babette as she gazed at the delicate white petals floating through the air and landing softly on the ground and in the stream.

"Well, it's home," said Ikiko. "Go sit on the grass by the stream. I'll bring some fruit."

The friends settled themselves on the grass, and a few moments later, the old man reappeared with a bowl of cherries, oranges and plums, which they dove into hungrily. As they began eating, Ikiko began talking.

"What is poetry?" he asked.

"Poetry," he answered himself, "is a lot like concentrated soup mix. If you try to eat the mix straight, you don't really get the flavor of the soup. So you usually have to add something—like water, or chicken stock, maybe some chopped onions or celery, maybe some extra spices, salt and pepper to taste."

Bridget wiped plum juice off her chin and wrinkled up her forehead in confusion. "I have no idea what you are talking about."

"Yes, well, I'll try again," said Ikiko. "Poetry is very *concentrated* language. Do you know what that means? It means that every word is important and powerful. One short poem can mean as much as an entire movie or story. But to understand poetry, the people who read it have to bring something of their own to it. Like adding water to concentrated soup mix, people must bring their own experiences and feelings to a poem. Only then can they really taste it."

"I get it," said Barnaby. "Like one little packet of fruit-punch powder can make a whole pitcher of red drink!"

"Sort of," nodded Ikiko. "But let me return to our soup example: What if you, Bridget, decided to add milk instead of water to the soup mix, and you, Babette, decided to use water, but add some carrots?"

"Our soups would be quite different, but with some things in common," answered Babette.

"Yes, that is correct. You both used the same soup mix, but brought different ingredients to it. And if Barnaby had nothing to add to the soup mix?"

"I guess he'd go hungry," giggled Bridget.

"In a way, he would," agreed Ikiko. "My point is, poetry is a very personal sort of language. It is personal to the people who read it, because they supply the 'water' of their feelings. And it is personal to the poet, the one who creates the poem, because the poet must concentrate his own personal 'soup' of experiences into a poem. But it is the beauty of poetry that it can be personal to a large number of people, even people with different backgrounds from different countries from different centuries."

"I thought poetry was just a bunch of boring rhymes," said Bridget. "You know, 'Roses are red, violets are blue, tape is sticky, and so is glue.' Aren't there a bunch of rules? It has to rhyme, right?"

"There are many different forms of poetry," explained Ikiko. "Even thousands of years ago, when poetry was just spoken and not written, people still used certain forms. And these forms are like tools that help poets focus their writing. You see, if there are rules to stick to, you have to focus and try harder to get your message across. But before I show you how to write your own poetry, why don't we go over some of the basic terms and forms so we will all understand each other?"

Babette, Bridget, and Barnaby all nodded. Beauregard was off staring at the glistening, fat fish that packed the stream, but no one was paying any attention to him.

"Good," said Ikiko. "Now, there are so many terms and forms out there, it would take me forever to go over them all. Besides, I intend to show you how to *write* poetry, not write *about* poetry. The following are the high points."

An Overview of Poetic Terms

Rhyme

For words to rhyme, they have to have the same ending sounds. They don't have to have the same number of syllables, though. Here are some examples: bed/head, tiring/inspiring, spoken/broken, foes/suppose.

Sometimes poets use near rhymes, also called off rhymes, such as ponder/wonder, bliss/is, little/middle.

Rhythm

Rhythm in poetry is like rhythm in music—It's made up of beats and pauses. The rhythm of a poem can sometimes communicate as much as the words themselves. In poetry, rhythm is made through the pronunciation, punctuation, and word placement. Try reading this last part of Edgar Allan Poe's "The Raven" out loud:

> And the Raven, never flitting, still is sitting, still is
> sitting
> On the pallid bust of Pallas just above my
> chamber door;
> And his eyes have all the seeming of a demon's
> that is dreaming,
> And the lamplight o'er him streaming throws his
> shadow on the floor;
> And my soul from out that shadow that lies
> floating on the floor
> Shall be lifted—nevermore!

Do you hear the rhythm? A beat like DA-dum DA-dum DA-dum DA-dum?

Now read out loud these lines from Oscar Wilde's "The Ballad of Reading Gaol."

> Yet each man kills the thing he loves,
> By each let this be heard,
> Some do it with a bitter look,
> Some with a flattering word.

That poem has a different beat, more like da-DUM da-DUM da-DUM da-DUM. These are the two most common rhythms in poetry.

There are others, of course. Have you ever heard these lines?

> And I heard him exclaim as he rode out of sight:
> "Merry Christmas to all, and to all a good night."

That's more like da-da-DUM da-da-DUM da-da-DUM da-da-DUM.

Now try reading this:

> Coffee and crumpets and butter with jelly,
> Bacon and pancakes to fill up my belly.

That sounds like DA-dum-dum DA-dum-dum DA-dum-dum, doesn't it?

The important thing about rhythm is that it's one of the things that gives poetry its musical quality and its power. Everyday speech has a rhythm (try listening to it), but we aren't usually aware of it. Poets, on the other hand, have a sharp ear for rhythm and harness it to make their poems stronger.

Verse

Verse is the proper term for a line of poetry.

Stanza

A stanza is a group of verses thought of as one piece of a poem. In this example from Samuel Coleridge's "The Rime of the Ancient Mariner," each stanza is made up of four lines.

> All in a hot and copper sky,
> The bloody Sun, at noon,
>
> Right up above the mast did stand,
> No bigger than the Moon.
>
> Day after day, day after day,
> We stuck, nor breath nor motion;
> As idle as a painted ship
> Upon a painted ocean.
>
> Water, water, everywhere,
> And all the boards did shrink;
> Water, water, everywhere,
> Nor any drop to drink.
>
> The very deep did rot: O Christ!
> That ever this should be!
> Yea, slimy things did crawl with legs
> Upon the slimy sea.

Stanzas don't always have to be the same length. Look at this poem by Carl Sandburg.

HARVEST

When the corn stand yellow in September,
A red flower ripens and shines among the stalks
And a red silk creeps among the broad ears
And tall tassels lift over all else
                    and keep a singing
                    to the prairies
                    and the wind.

          They are the grand lone ones
          For they are never saved
                    along with the corn:

                    They are cut down
                    and piled high
                    and burned.

                    Their fire
                    lights the west in November.

Here the poem has no set stanza length. The first
stanza has seven verses, the second and third have
three, and the fourth has two.

Different types of poems have different rules for
stanza length (we'll talk about forms in a minute) but,
in general, stanzas are the chunks of a poem set apart
from the other chunks by space.

Assonance

Assonance is the repetition of the same or similar vowel sounds in a passage. Listen to the long "i" sounds in these opening lines from John Keats's "Ode on a Grecian Urn."

> Thou still unravish'd bride of quietness,
> Thou foster-child of silence and slow time

Do you hear the "i" sound in *bride, quietness, child, silence,* and *time*?

Now try reading these lines from "The Love Song of J. Alfred Prufrock," by T. S. Eliot, and listen for the "i" and "e" sounds.

> Let us go then, you and I,
> When the evening is spread out against the sky
> Like a patient etherised upon a table;
> Let us go, through certain half-deserted streets,
> The muttering retreats
> Of restless nights in one-night cheap hotels

You can hear the "i" in *I, sky, etherised,* and *night,* and you can hear the "e" in *evening, etherised, streets, retreats,* and *cheap.*

Here's one more example. See if you hear the "o" sounds in these lines from "Blood-Sister," by Adrienne Rich.

> Shoring up the ocean. A railroad track
> ran close to the coast for miles
> through the potato-fields, bringing us
> to summer.

Assonance makes poetry sing. To make use of it in your poems, start listening to the music in the words you hear. Say them to yourself. Sometimes the hidden music of a certain word can stir up more feelings than another word with the same meaning. Listen with your ears and your feelings.

Alliteration

Alliteration is the repetition of a beginning consonant sound in a text. Alliteration is often used in newspaper headlines and advertisements because it's catchy and easy to remember—like "Boggs Bats Better Bald" or "Dynamo Destroys Dirt."

In poetry alliteration is used for emphasis. Look at this poem by e. e. cummings (he never capitalized his name—aren't poets weird?) called "All in Green Went My Love Riding." It is filled with both alliteration and assonance.

All in green went my love riding
on a great horse of gold
into the silver dawn.

four lean hounds crouched low and smiling
the merry deer ran before.

Fleeter be they than dappled dreams
the swift sweet deer
the red rare deer.

Four red roebuck at a white water
the cruel bugle sang before.

Horn at hip went my love riding
riding the echo down
into the silver dawn.

four lean hounds crouched low and smiling
the level meadows ran before.

Softer be they than slippered sleep
the lean lithe deer
the fleet flown deer.

Four fleet does at a gold valley
the famished arrow sang before.

Bow at belt went my love riding
riding the mountain down
into the silver dawn.

four lean hounds crouched low and smiling
the sheer peaks ran before.

Paler be they than daunting death
the sleek slim deer
the tall tense deer.

Four tall stags at a green mountain
the lucky hunter sang before.

All in green went my love riding
on a great horse of gold
into the silver dawn.

four lean hounds crouched low and smiling
my heart fell dead before.

Alliteration helps make poetry memorable, like the
beat of a song you can't get out of your head.
Alliteration is like the sound of a cymbal accenting
the poem's beat.

Beauregard says poetry and music are
related (in case you hadn't noticed).
Musicians and poets both have keen ears
for the sound and rhythm of words. For
instance, rap music is loaded with
assonance and alliteration, and rap
musicians are great at using these effects
together with rhythm to create powerful
songs. Listen to the words of your favorite
songs—you'll find they have a lot in common with
poetry.

Simile and Metaphor

You probably already know what similes and
metaphors are, but we'll review them anyway. A
simile is a comparison between two things that uses
the word *like* or *as*—for example, "her tears fell like
rain" or "his eyes were as bright as the noonday sun."
A metaphor is a comparison made by describing one
thing *as* another—for example, "the march of the
army was a drumbeat heard throughout the
countryside" or "the sky is a majestic canopy fretted
with golden fire."

Similes and metaphors in poems can be simple observations, or they can be very complicated. They can be used to paint a picture or make a point. Poets usually put a lot of thought into the comparisons they make, so when reading poetry, ask yourself what exactly the poet is trying to say. Here's an example of a simile from Ezra Pound's "The Garden."

> Like a skein of loose silk blown against a wall
> She walks by the railing of a path in Kensington
> Gardens

This simile compares a woman to a piece of silk blown against a wall. Think about what silk is like. its beautiful, fragile, light, thin. The wind in the simile is rough with the silk—it blows it against a wall. The woman in this poem is precious and fine but is surrounded by threatening forces. See how using a simile brings so much descriptive power to these two lines?

Here's a fairly simple metaphor that opens the poem "The Goose-Girl" by Edna St. Vincent Millay.

> Spring rides no horses down the hill,
> But comes on foot, a goose-girl still.

The poet is saying that spring is honest and simple, like a goose-girl, not like a rich person who would ride on a horse.

But metaphors can be more complicated. Read this section of a poem by Lawrence Ferlinghetti and see if you can figure out what comparison he is making.

> Just as I used to say
>   love comes harder to the aged
> because they've been running
>   on the same old rails too long
> and then when the sly switch comes along
>   they miss the turn
> and burn up the wrong rail while
>   the gay caboose goes flying
>   and the steamengine driver don't recognize
>   them new electric horns

Throughout the poem, older people are described as railroad cars that go down the wrong track. The poet makes the comparison without ever coming right out and saying "old people are like trains," but you can see it anyway.

Word Placement

When we talk about word placement, we don't just mean the order in which words appear. The length of each line, where it begins —next to the left margin? in the middle? on the right margin?—and the arrangement of lines on the page make a difference to how a poem is read.

Many poets, especially modern poets, arrange their lines in order to create certain effects. In the Ferlinghetti poem, did you notice how the line arrangement made you pause in some places and speed up in others? e.e. cummings is also known for his careful word placement, even jamming several words together or breaking words apart to make a picture or create a rhythm.

Read this poem by cummings.

Buffalo Bill's
defunct
                who used to
                ride a watersmooth-silver
                                        stallion
and break onetwothreefourfive pigeonsjustlikethat
                                                Jesus
he was a handsome man
                        and what i want to know is
how do you like your blueeyed boy
Mister Death

There are no rules regarding word placement, and
it can be as powerful as rhyme or rhythm. If you
decide to experiment with it, always do it for a
reason—don't just scatter your lines across a page.

✎ ✎ ✎ ✎ ✎

Bridget, Babette, and Barnaby all sat silently,
starry-eyed, smiling to themselves. It seemed
as if they were soaking up their surroundings
more than they had before—the feel of the soft
grass beneath them, the smell of the plum
blossoms, the sound of the stream.

"Ahem," said Ikiko, clearing his throat to get
their attention. "As I was saying, there are
more forms and terms in poetry than you can
imagine. Petrarchan sonnets, Shakespearean
sonnets, Alexandrines, ballad stanzas, ottava

rima, iambic pentameter, and on and on. There will be time enough for you to learn about these things in your literature classes when you study other people's poetry. The terms I have just gone over with you are meant to open your eyes to the possibilities of your own poetry."

Beauregard says you can see from the examples Ikiko gave that there are many different kinds of poems on many different topics. If you want to learn more about the different forms, pick up an **anthology** of poetry from your library or bookstore. An anthology is a collection of writings by different authors. A good anthology of poetry can help you figure out what kinds of poetry you like.

✍ EXERCISE #8 ✍
Time to Rhyme

Write down at least three words that rhyme with each of the following words.

1. red _____

2. cape _____

3. gloom _____

4. chase _____

5. valentine _____

6. bored _____

7. hitches _____

8. river _____

9. flaring _____

10. beef _____

✍ QUIZ #9 ✍
I Got Rhythm!

In each of the following passages, draw a line under the accented (stressed) syllables. This is a difficult exercise, but don't get discouraged. Just do your best. Check out the example below.

> T<u>y</u>ger, <u>ty</u>ger: <u>burn</u>ing <u>bright</u>
> <u>In</u> the <u>for</u>ests <u>of</u> the <u>night</u>.

1. I set her on my pacing steed,
   And nothing else saw all day long,
   For sidelong would she bend, and sing
   A faery's song.

2. Because I could not stop for Death,
   He kindly stopped for me;
   The carriage held but just ourselves
   And Immortality.

3. For the moon never beams without
   bringing me dreams
   Of the beautiful Annabel Lee;
   And the stars never rise but I feel the
   bright eyes
   Of the beautiful Annabel Lee;

4. One if by land and two if by sea
   And I on the opposite shore will be,
   Ready to ride and spread the alarm
   Through every Middlesex village
   and farm.

5. "The time has come," the Walrus said,
      "To talk of many things:
   Of shoes—and ships—and sealing-wax—
      Of cabbages—and kings—
   And why the sea is boiling hot—
      And whether pigs have wings."

✍ QUIZ #10 ✍
Can You Stand the Assonance?

In the following passages identify the vowel
sound or sounds that are repeated and write
them in the blank provided. Then underline
the syllables that have those vowel sounds.

____ 1. I met a traveler from an antique land
      Who said: Two vast and trunkless legs
      of stone
      Stand in the desert . . .

____ 2. Leave no black plume as a token of that
      lie thy soul hath spoken!
      Leave my loneliness unbroken!—quit
      the bust above my door!

____ 3. He took his vorpal sword in hand:
      Long time the manxome foe he
      sought—

____ 4. Let others freeze with angling reeds,
      And cut their legs with shells and
      weeds.

____ 5. I stand amid the roar
      Of a surf-tormented shore.

✍ QUIZ #11 ✍
A Little Alliteration

Identify the alliteration in the following passages. Write down which consonant or consonants are repeated at the beginning of words in the passage in the blank provided, and then underline the words that begin with that consonant.

_____ 1. Cold are the crabs that crawl on yonder hills,
Colder the cucumbers that grow beneath.

_____ 2. Pale, beyond porch and portal,
Crowned with calm leaves she stands
Who gathers all things mortal
With cold immortal hands.

_____ 3. Deep into that darkness peering, long I stood there wondering,
fearing,
Doubting, dreaming dreams no mortal ever dared to dream before

_____ 4. The flowers do fade, and wanton fields
To wayward winter reckoning yields.

_____ 5. Time drives the flocks from field to fold,
When rivers rage, and rocks grow cold . . .

"But Ikiko, we're just kids," Bridget protested. "I really want to write poems now, but the ones you showed us were all written by grown-ups who know a lot more than we do. I can't write like that."

"I certainly hope not," chuckled Ikiko. "Remember, poetry is very personal. You should never try to copy another poet's style. As for being too young, well, that's nonsense. Do you have eyes? Do you have ears? Do you have feelings?"

"Yes, but . . . "

"No buts!" thundered Ikiko. Then, calming himself again, he continued, "It is true, adults have more life experiences they can bring to poems. But the older you get, the more set in your ways you tend to become. You start looking at things the way you *expect* them to be instead of using fresh eyes to really observe. The world becomes duller. Young people can see and feel things adults cannot. That's why young people make wonderful poets. In fact, most people who go on to become famous poets when they grow up started writing poetry when they were quite young."

"Really?" said Barnaby enthusiastically.

"Yes, really," Ikiko assured him. "And to prove it, I'm going to show you some examples of very impressive poems written by young people. In a little while, that is. Is that acceptable?"

Barnaby, Babette, and Bridget nodded in agreement.

Beauregard says poets can achieve greatness at a young age. Many poets whose work students read and study in school wrote some of their best poems while they were still teenagers! Here are some of them:

Arthur Rimbaud, a French poet, wrote one of his most impressive poems, "The Drunken Boat," when he was sixteen. He wrote his masterpiece, "A Season in Hell," when he was nineteen.

Edna St. Vincent Millay began writing poetry in high school, and her college education was paid for by a wealthy admirer of her poems.

Langston Hughes, a central figure in what's known as the Harlem Renaissance, began writing poems at eighteen and became one of America's most respected African American poets.

"Good," he said. "Now I told you we were not going to spend time working on specific kinds of poetry, just on sharpening up your poetic skills in general. I meant that, but to do it, I'm going to teach you about one kind of poem called **haiku.** Writing haiku is a good way to stimulate your poetic senses. Remember how I told you poetry is concentrated language? Well, haiku are some of the most concentrated of all poems."

HAIKU: QUICK SKETCHES OF FEELING

"Haiku was developed in Japan hundreds of years ago," explained Ikiko. "Each haiku, or poem, is only seventeen syllables long, but good haiku pack a big punch. Every word must be carefully chosen to capture the feeling or event the poet wants to portray.

"The seventeen syllables of a haiku are traditionally broken into three unrhymed lines: the first line has five syllables, the second line has seven syllables, and the third line has five syllables. Think it's impossible to get any message across with those tight restrictions? Look at these examples from the Japanese masters."

> Mother lost, long gone . . .
> At the deep, dark sea I stare . . .
> At the deep, dark sea.
>
> Issa

Even with insects . . .
Some are hatched out musical,
Some, alas, tone deaf.

Issa

Moon in the water:
Broken and broken again,
And still it is there.

Choshu

I'm very sorry
To have to die at this time
With plum trees in bloom.

Raizan

"See how the poets pack so much into each word?" said Ikiko. "The first poem by Issa is very sad, a poem about the loss of a loved one, but he doesn't have to rant and moan to reveal his feelings—instead he simply mentions the deep, dark sea. How does thinking about the deep, dark sea make you feel? Small? Lost? Cold? Weak? But Issa's second poem is more of an observation, a comparison between the talents of humans and insects.

"What about Choshu's poem? He is only looking at the reflection of the moon in the water, but he has created a sense of wonder about the grandeur, age, and beauty of the moon."

"Hey, wait a minute," said Barnaby, suddenly realizing something. "You write haiku, too, don't you? What was that you said when you first found us . . .?"

"He said, 'I have visitors, Snowflakes unmuddied by earth: A gift from the sky,' if I remember right," said Babette.

"Yes, you remember quite correctly," said Ikiko, obviously pleased. "And you are correct as well, Barnaby. That was a haiku. It was my impression of your arrival."

Barnaby and Babette smiled broadly.

"What I want you to do now is give me *your* impressions. Don't worry if your poems don't sound like the examples I gave—they're *your* poems, after all. Now I want you to write five haiku. Take your time. You don't have to write them all at once."

✍ EXERCISE #9 ✍
Write a Few Haiku

Write one haiku on each of the following subjects.

1. A season. Pick any season and think about how it makes you feel or about something that happens during that season—like riding your bike in the summer, or the sound of crunching on dead leaves in the fall, or being warm in bed when it's snowing outside in winter, or rainy days in spring. These are only suggestions. Try to think of what *you* feel during each season.

2. School. Choose anything that has to do with school: waking up in the morning, waiting for the bell to let you out at the end of the day, doing homework.

3. Being alone. What do you do when you are by yourself? Do you feel happy or lonely? What do you think about? Are you bored?

4. Being with friends. Think about your friends. How does being with them make you feel? Write about one particular friend, if you want, or about what you do when you're with your friends.

5. Home. How do you feel when you are at home? Do you miss your home when you

aren't there? Who lives with you and how do they make you feel? How do you feel about your home town?

 **Beauregard says** writers need inspiration. I'll bet there isn't a poet in the world who could sit down and write a poem without inspiration. Inspiration is anything that excites your mind or tickles your creativity. For some people, taking a long walk by themselves is inspiring. For others, it's reading the newspaper or listening to music. But most of the time, inspiration just strikes you, all of a sudden. You might just be taking a bath, or getting into bed, or riding a bus when—wham!—a great idea hits you.

Poets throughout history have given credit to a "muse" for those breakthrough ideas (muses were originally thought of as goddesses who help artists, remember?). But wherever it comes from, the important thing is to grab hold of your inspiration when you get it. Write down your idea as quickly as you can so you don't lose it! Some great ideas come only once.

✎ ✎ ✎ ✎ ✎

"Ow," grumbled Bridget, rubbing her temple. "My brain hurts. Writing haiku is hard!"

"Yes, it is, especially for a beginner," agreed Ikiko. "That's because it is such a strict format. But as I said, sticking to a strict format helps you focus and helps strengthen your creativity. What do you think? Are you starting to feel like a poet?"

"Oh, yes!" Bridget replied, nodding her head vigorously.

"What about you two? Are you feeling creative?" Ikiko asked Barnaby and Babette. They both nodded eagerly.

"Good," said the teacher. "That means we can have some fun now. Remember, Bridget, how you complained that all the poems I talked about were written by adults? Well, now I'm going to show you what kids—some of them even younger than you—can do."

YOUNG POETS SPEAK OUT

THE SUNBEAMS

Sun, Sun do you know
You are beams in the flames,
With glowworms in the light
And bright yellow red
Sharp silver flames
Spinning up,
Like a big block of gold
The sun is a very magic fellow.

Linda Pidgeon, age 7

LOST

He lost it over the dark gray hills
Of wonder —
Where the fingerless oaks grow;
Where the fruitless orange groves blow
In the merciless
Hungry
      Wind.

It must, by now,
Be torn
Between
The lush brown Earth
And the raging winter sky.

The wind must have
Dragged it
Over Moors,
Fields and Mountains
While he was at home
Enjoying his pipe.

        Eve Recht, age 11

A STORM AT SEA

A storm at sea is dangerous.
The wind blows as if it has
           no sympathy.
The sky suddenly darkens—
A slash of lightning crosses
         the sky.

Then a sound like a giant
Stamping his foot
            in anger.
A spray of tiny stars would
            come from the waves—
Huge blue-green hands
            with white fingers
Rise from the sea.

Delia Valentin, age 10

YOUTH

We stood together
Hand in hand.
He, so earnest, so concerned
In my tears.
Why do I cry?
What questions he asks!
Why do I cry?
How can I tell?

I could have laughed.
I could have stood
And screamed
At the dull drips of rain,
His fond stupidity.
His wiry hair,
His youth.
But no,
I stand and cry.

Anonymous, age 13

UNTITLED

The full moon whispered to the world
A word of wonder.
Then unfurled the light which lit the land
And lured the owls up to its hand.

John Rathe, age 12

BREEZE

Gentle as a feather
Cat quiet
Snow soft
Gentle, gentle as a feather
Softer than snow
Quiet as a cat
Comes
The evening breeze.

Marie Hourigan, age 11

Barnaby, Babette, and Bridget all smiled, proud of the poems written by people their own ages. Even Beauregard stopped stalking the shiny fish long enough to come and hear the poems. Ikiko smiled, too, but for reasons of his own.

"So, do you all feel like writers now?" he asked, somewhat slyly.

"Oh, yes," replied Babette. "After all you have taught us, I feel like a writer."

"Me, too," Bridget chimed in. "I just know I can write."

"I feel the same way," Barnaby added. "Now that I know . . ."

"Stop!" shouted Ikiko, raising his hand to silence them. "You are wrong. You are not writers yet because, if you want to be considered writers, you must stick to a very important rule. . . ."

"Did you hear what I heard?" Bridget said to her friends.

"And the rule is . . . ," continued Ikiko.

"Quick, pick up your notebooks, guys!" urged Barnaby.

RULE #4
Writers write or, in other words, writers who do not write are not writers.

Barnaby looked confused. "What kind of rule is that?" he asked. "That's as confusing as some of those haiku Bridget wrote."

"Hey!" Bridget objected.

"Enough, you two," said Ikiko. "The rule is very simple. In your life you will meet many people who will tell you that they are writers or poets or artists or actors. I do not know the rules for actors, but I do know that it's all well and good to claim that you have the ability to write, but you are not a writer unless you *do* something with that ability.

"So if you want to be a writer, *write*. It doesn't matter what—poems or articles or essays or stories or . . ."

"Wait a sec, Ikiko," said Bridget. "We don't know anything about stories. I can deal with poems and articles and essays, but no one has told us *anything* about stories."

"I see," said Ikiko, somewhat shocked. He shook his head and shrugged. "Poetry is usually one of the last things a quester learns, but you seem to have skipped a step. I'd love to give you some more exercises, but you really must be on your way. You've still much to learn and you have to make it back to Paris in time to save the café."

Ikiko got up off the ground and brushed off his robe, although it didn't really need brushing. Looking up in the sky, he wrinkled up his face into a squint.

"Judging from the sun, it seems to be about three o'clock. If you hurry, you can make it down to the docks in time to catch the freighter. It should take you where you need to go."

The kids got up, stretched, and were getting ready to go when a terrible yowl followed by a loud splash broke into the peaceful surroundings. When they turned toward the stream to see what had caused the racket, they saw Beauregard, looking very silly with his fur all stuck to his body, climbing out of the water onto the bank.

"What is the matter, Beauregard? Did you slip?" asked Babette.

"More likely he wanted to get friendly with one of the carp," chuckled Ikiko. "That stream is much deeper than it looks, I'm afraid."

Beauregard gave a little sniff, shook himself, and tried to look innocent and dignified at the same time.

Bridget laughed and turned to their host. "I guess we'd better get moving. Which way to the docks?"

Ikiko pointed west, toward the yellowing sun. After giving each of the travelers some plums and oranges, he sent them down the path to the docks. Beauregard walked along beside them as if nothing had happened.

They hadn't gone very far when Barnaby stopped. "You guys go ahead. I forgot to tell Ikiko something," he said. "I'll catch up."

With that, he turned and ran back down the path before Babette or Bridget could say anything. A few minutes later, he came jogging back, just as they were reaching the docks.

"Well?" asked Bridget. "What did you tell him?"

"It just came to me," said Barnaby, blushing. "I told him this.

> Plums and oranges
> My friend gives me, and poems
> To fill my pockets.

"Well, well," smiled Babette. "I guess you are a writer now!"

Chapter 9

The Great Story Safari

Sure enough, that freighter Ikiko told us about was pulling into the dock just as we got there. The captain came ashore and Babette only had to mention Ikiko's name and the quest, and he said he'd give us free passage (which was certainly agreeable, because we didn't have any money). The kids all seemed caught up in their own thoughts once we were aboard the ship. Bridget just stared out to sea, and Babette and Barnaby wrote in their notebooks. That suited me fine, because my fur was a total mess. Something about hanging around with those three always gets me dunked in water more often than I like!

Anyway, I went off to a secluded, sunny part of the deck to take care of my fur. Trouble was, with the warm sun and the rocking of the waves, I fell asleep before I even finished licking my back paws. We were headed west, that's all I knew.

I have no idea how long I slept, but I was rudely awakened by the blasting of the ship's horn signaling that we were pulling toward shore—that and three pairs of hands shaking me in the roughest way!

✎ ✎ ✎ ✎ ✎

"Beauregard! Beauregard, wake up!" urged Babette.

"I thought cats were supposed to be light sleepers," mused Barnaby.

"There's nothing light about Beauregard," snickered Bridget.

With that, the cat's eyes sprang open. It even seemed like he shot a mean glance at Bridget. Apparently, Beauregard was sensitive about his weight.

"Uh, just kidding Beauregard," said Bridget. "I was just seeing if you were faking being asleep. Come on, we have to go now. We're here, wherever 'here' is."

"We are somewhere along the east coast of Africa, as far as I can tell," Barnaby offered.

Babette was impressed. "How do you know that?"

"Well, I noticed the angle of the sun, balanced it with the direction of the wind, corrected for seasonal differences, and . . . ummm . . . actually, the captain told me," he admitted, a little embarrassed. "But I was pretty sure it was Africa before he told me."

"Yeah, right," said Bridget. "Let's just get ashore and figure out what we're going to do, okay?"

Everyone agreed, so they got up, thanked the captain, and walked down the gangplank. The area around the dock was crammed with people: merchants selling their wares, family members waiting for loved ones to come off the ship, traders, and government inspectors. Slowly, the questers made their way through the noisy crowd. Soon they came upon a small, waterfront restaurant with a wide veranda shaded by a heavy roof of dried palm leaves.

The afternoon sun was so bright that it was hard to see into the restaurant, but as Bridget, Barnaby, Babette, and Beauregard came closer, they distinctly heard someone call out to them.

"Have you come to join the hunt, then?" It was a low, deep voice, full-chested but a little rough around the edges.

The travelers stopped and squinted toward the veranda. Through the semi-darkness they could make out the shadowy outline of a person sitting at a table along the back wall.

"Come on out of the heat and have a cold drink," invited the voice. "My treat."

Beauregard sniffed the air, checking for danger. Barnaby, Babette, and Bridget looked quizzically at each other, but since no one could come up with any objections and since having a cold drink sounded wonderful, they walked up the steps and onto the porch. After pausing for a second to let their eyes adjust to the light, they walked over to the table where the mysterious person sat, leaning back against the wall.

"Have a seat," crackled the person, whose face was shrouded in darkness beneath a wide-brimmed hat.

"Thank you," said Babette, always the first to remember her manners. "My name is Babette, and these are my friends Barnaby, Bridget, and Beauregard. We are on a quest for the Lost Art of Writing."

On hearing Babette's announcement, the shadowy person leaned forward so suddenly that the chair scraped against the ground and Barnaby, Bridget, Babette, and Beauregard all jumped back in fear.

"I'm sorry, I didn't mean to frighten you," chuckled the person. "It's just been so long since I've crossed paths with a quester. They used to come through all the time, but not anymore. Let me introduce myself—my name is Zenobia. I would be glad to guide you on this part of your journey."

The travelers could barely conceal their surprise. That deep, raspy voice belonged to a woman! Zenobia pulled off her hat to reveal coal-black hair neatly combed into a tight braid in back—coal black except for two large, white streaks at each temple, that is. Her face was dark, the color of coffee, and had a tough, leathery look about it, as if she had spent long days and nights exposed to the wind and sun. It was impossible to guess her age. She wore a loose white shirt and khaki pants and carried a long, curved knife tucked in her belt. Barnaby, Babette, and Bridget all gaped at her in awe. She seemed like a real adventurer!

Strangely, Beauregard seemed to be grinning. Zenobia gave him a barely noticeable nod and then turned her attention back to the others.

"Please, sit, sit," she urged them. The kids sat down, and she called into the restaurant for some refreshments. Once everyone was comfortably sipping an unidentifiable green, but very refreshing, drink, Zenobia began asking questions.

"So, you say you are on a quest for the Lost Art of Writing. Who sent you on this quest?" she asked.

"Well, we don't know his name," said Bridget. "It was the manager, or the head waiter, maybe, at the Mute Café in Paris. If we don't return to the café with the Rules of Good Writing, it will be washed away in a flood."

Zenobia's eyes widened a little. "I see," she mused. "Well, that must not happen. I would like to offer you lunch, but there's no time to

waste. Finish your drinks. I'll go see about supplies. We'll leave right away."

Zenobia stood up and put on her hat. She was a very tall, powerfully built woman with large hands and ropey muscles. Before anyone could ask her anything, she strode out into the sunlight. A few minutes later she returned, leading five horses behind her.

"Come on!" she yelled to them. "I hope you know how to ride."

In fact, neither Babette nor Barnaby had ever ridden a horse, and Bridget had only sat on one once at a state fair back home. They didn't dare tell Zenobia, though. There was something about her that wouldn't take no for an answer. Strangely enough, Beauregard looked perfectly comfortable with the idea of riding, and he scampered out to get first pick of the horses.

When the questers walked out, Zenobia and Beauregard were already mounted on their steeds, and *they seemed to be having a conversation!* Before any of them could even open their mouths to ask questions about this new surprise, though, Zenobia hopped down and handed them all wide-brimmed hats just like hers (Bridget put hers on top of her baseball cap, so she was especially shaded) and gave them each a canteen, which they hung across their bodies with wide straps. After helping the three kids onto their horses, she leaped up on hers and took the lead. Bridget, Babette, and Barnaby were all very relieved when their horses naturally began to follow Zenobia's, without any command from them.

No one spoke for a while, but as they approached the outskirts of town, Barnaby finally worked up the courage to ask her what her plan was and where they were going.

"We're going on a safari!" she yelled excitedly. "Do you know what a safari is? It's an adventure, an expedition, a journey, a hunt. And we are going on a great story safari!"

WHY DO PEOPLE LIKE STORIES?

Zenobia kept her eyes forward, but she talked at length to the questers as they rode out into the grassy plains.

"Stories are as old as language itself. As soon as people figured out how to string a few words together, they were sitting around the campfire telling each other stories. In every country in the world, myths, fables, legends, fairytales—some based on fact, some pure imagination—have been passed down, generation after generation, for thousands of years," she said. "Some stories are known the entire world over, some only in certain villages and towns. Stories help make us what we are. Stories are our history—because what is history, after all? It's not a collection of dates and battles and treaties. History is a web of events and lives and deeds from the past.

"Stories can teach you, inspire you, entertain you. They can make you happy, or sad, or downright angry. Stories are important, and storytellers have a key role in any civilization because they help define it."

Zenobia paused to let what she had said sink in. Glancing over her shoulder at the confused faces behind her, she could tell that she had not quite gotten her message across.

"Babette!" she barked. "Tell me what you know about the story of King Arthur."

Babette was startled by Zenobia's thundering command, but she recovered quickly. "Well, er, according to legend, King Arthur was a great ruler of England a long, long time ago. He pulled a sword named Excalibur from a stone, which nobody else could do, and that made him king. Arthur gathered the best knights in the land to serve him, including the very best knight, Sir Lancelot, who was from France, of course, and they all sat at the Round Table. They went on a quest, just like us, except it was a quest for the Holy Grail. Arthur married Guinevere, who tragically fell in love with Lancelot. Their love . . ."

"That's enough!" said Zenobia. "I see you know the story. But tell me, in single words only, what the story is about."

"In single words?" Babette frowned. "How about honor? love? betrayal? duty? faith?"

"Very good," Zenobia replied. "Honor, love, betrayal, duty, faith. Those are things that have

been around a long time, don't you think?
People are still pretty concerned about them.
That's why this story endures. That's why it
keeps getting told in books and movies over
and over. It's a doozie of a story, for one thing,
and people still get something out of it six
hundred years after it first made it big."

Beauregard says what's up with
Zenobia? By now you've probably
figured out that Zenobia and I already
know each other. Of course, she
wasn't always a safari leader, and the
last time I saw her, she didn't have
those bits of white in her hair. To tell
you the truth, I'm not really sure where
she came from originally, but she did
tell me once she was from the royal
family of a fierce, war-like people, and that she ran
away because she got sick of fighting. Make no
mistake, though, Zenobia's no ninny. She was one of
the toughest undercover agents I ever worked with
while I was spying for the Elephant Empire.

Anyway, as she said, it had been a long time
since she'd met a quester, so she was a little rusty on
her story safari skills. I'll be coming in from time to
time to help her out with examples and comments, so
be on the lookout.

"Now, Bridget, have you ever heard of *The
Adventures of Huckleberry Finn*?" Zenobia
asked. "The story of a young boy and his
travels on the Mississippi River . . ."

"Oh, sure," Bridget piped in enthusiastically. "It's about freedom and friendship and fun and adventure!"

"Absolutely!" agreed Zenobia. "Is it any wonder that people still love this story more than a hundred years after it was written? And Barnaby—unless I miss my guess, you are a scientist. What do you think of the story of Frankenstein, that brilliant scientist who brought the dead back to life? Why does that story keep getting told?"

"Because it's a fantastic story!" cried Barnaby. "It's about death and loss and dangerous pride, and loneliness and fear and revenge!"

"Well, that's certainly enough to keep people coming back, even nearly two hundred years after the story was first unleashed. Death, pride, and revenge certainly seem to be basic human emotions. What is my point in asking you about these stories, you're wondering? I just want to show you how stories reflect human experience. By reading stories, people learn more about their own lives and the lives of others."

Beauregard says you never may have heard of the stories Zenobia mentions. If not, you might want to check them out at the library. One very good book about King Arthur is *The Book of Merlin* by T. H. White. Merlin is a magician who is Arthur's advisor and tutor.

The Adventures of Huckleberry Finn was written by Mark Twain. Oddly enough, Mark Twain also wrote a book called *A Connecticut Yankee at King Arthur's Court*, about a man who travels back in time to King Arthur's realm.

Frankenstein was written by Mary Shelley. It's a short book, but it is very scary, so don't read it late at night!

Bridget nodded slowly and sadly. "I see that. But we are here to learn to write stories, aren't we? I don't think I will ever be able to write a story like *Huckleberry Finn*. I mean, where did the idea for that story come from? How would I find an idea for a story?"

"I'm glad you asked that, Bridget," said Zenobia, smiling encouragingly.

FINDING STORY IDEAS: YOUR LIFE IS YOUR SOURCE

"Do you think that when the authors of the stories we just talked about sat down to write, they said to themselves, 'I'm going to write a big, important story that people will read for generations'?" Zenobia asked. "Probably not. Most writers draw on personal experience to create their stories. They write what they know."

"You mean Mary Shelley, the woman who wrote *Frankenstein*, actually *knew* a scientist who brought dead bodies back to life?" yelped Barnaby.

"No, I seriously doubt that," replied Zenobia. "But she was very familiar with the feelings you described: fear, loss, loneliness. The events in her life made her capable of creating such a monster—on paper, that is.

"And Mark Twain, who created Huckleberry Finn, actually was a riverboat captain on the Mississippi for a time, so many of Huck's adventures are derived from Twain's personal experience. You see, by writing what you know, by using your own life as a source of information, you make your stories real to the people who read them. Ever notice how good stories, even though you know they are made up, seem real and believable? That's because the writers put their own lives and feelings on the page."

Bridget sniffed. "But I don't know anything! Nothing interesting ever happens to me."

Without turning around, Zenobia reined in her horse and stopped dead still. All the other horses stopped too. Barnaby and Babette shifted uncomfortably in their saddles. Beauregard sniffed the air uneasily. Then, very slowly, their safari leader turned to face them.

"You silly, silly girl!" she growled. "Nothing ever happens to you, eh? Have you forgotten so soon how to use your eyes and ears? Can't you see past the end of your nose? Life is happening to you all the time! Events are unfolding as we speak! Look!"

Babette, Bridget, and Barnaby looked in the direction Zenobia was pointing. A sleek yellow lioness crouched low in the grass, eyeing an antelope, waiting. The questers felt afraid, but excited—afraid for the antelope, excited for the lioness.

"Now look there!" cried Zenobia, pointing toward a large lake in the distance. And just as she pointed, a huge, beautiful, pink cloud rose from the lake and covered the sky. No, not a cloud—flamingos! Thousands and thousands of huge, pink birds swarmed through the sky.

The beating of their wings distracted the antelope for a moment and the lioness pounced, barely missing her prey. The antelope ran for its life with the determined hunter in pursuit. Bridget, Babette, and Barnaby watched in wonder until the animals disappeared over a small hill.

"That's what I call *something*!" gasped Bridget.

"Well, I hope it opened your eyes, at least," said Zenobia, tapping her horse with her heels and getting the whole procession moving again. "But important events in your life aren't always as obvious as half million flamingos taking flight at once. Not by a long shot. That's why you have to keep sharp and use those powers of observation. In fact, I'll bet you kids have stumbled through your lives without a second thought as to how you are growing or how things around you are changing."

"That may have been true before, but not now," argued Babette. "We are learning to observe."

"Good," grinned Zenobia. "Then try this exercise for me."

✍ EXERCISE #10 ✍
Writing What You Know

1. Think of a time when you were really afraid—the most terrified you have ever been. We're not talking about being scared in a horror movie, because you know that those aren't real. Write one paragraph about the experience—why you were afraid, what you were afraid of, and how it felt.

2. Think about your biggest disappointment or failure. Did you ever really believe in something or someone, and then get let down badly? Were you ever looking forward to something, only to have it denied? Did you ever try as hard as you could to do something, but not be able to? Write one paragraph about the experience.

3. What was your happiest experience with your whole family? Do you remember a certain event or day in which the whole family came together and felt happy? It doesn't have to be any special holiday— maybe it was just one meal, or a time you went to the movies together. Write a paragraph about the happiest experience you have shared with your family.

4. Do you remember feeling proud of yourself for something you accomplished? Think

about the most pleased you've ever been with yourself. Maybe it was finally beating older brother at checkers. Maybe it was getting the training wheels taken off your bike. Maybe it was playing a song on the piano without messing up once. Write a paragraph about your proudest moment.

5. Think about the end of something in your life. If your family has moved, think about the last time you were in your old house. How did you feel, knowing you'd never be in the house again? Maybe you used to be friends with someone who has moved away. How did you feel the last time you saw that person? What was it like? How did you feel on the last day of summer vacation? On the last day of school? Pick one of these topics—or any ending you can think of in your life—and write a paragraph about the experience.

GETTING READY TO WRITE

"So you see, your life is filled with significant moments," said Zenobia with great satisfaction. "You have lived many events that would help you write a story."

Bridget, Babette, and Barnaby now all seemed a little more at ease with the idea of story writing, but they still had their doubts.

"Does that mean that when I write a story, I have to write only what happens to me? I can't make things up? That's not a story!" cried Barnaby.

"I was sad and scared when I got separated from my parents once, but that story doesn't seem as interesting as *Frankenstein*!" protested Bridget.

Zenobia sighed. "I see I should define some terms and make some clarifications. You'll have to forgive me for rambling. As I said, it's been a long time since I've crossed paths with a quester. Let's take this step by step. First, let's go over some definitions."

Some Important Terms

Prose—Prose is any writing that's not poetry. When you write a report, that's prose. When you read a textbook or story, that's prose.

Fiction—Fiction is made up. That is, fiction is any writing that is not completely factual or any text based on the author's imagination. You'll find that many books and stories take place in real locations and mention real people, and sometimes the people in the stories are based on real people, but if the author makes *anything* up, then the story is fiction. The opposite of fiction is nonfiction, which is factual writing (like a report or a newspaper article).

Plot—The plot in a story is the chain of events, or the storyline. The plot is what happens. In "Cinderella", for example, the plot is as follows: a girl who lives with her evil stepsisters and stepmother gets visited by her fairy godmother, who uses her magic to make a beautiful gown and coach for Cinderella to use to go to the royal ball. The only catch is that she has to be back home by midnight, before the magic wears off. The handsome prince falls in love with her at the ball, but she has to run out when the clock starts chiming midnight. The prince doesn't know her name, but luckily she accidentally leaves behind a glass slipper, and the prince goes around the kingdom trying it on every woman's foot until he finds the one it fits, which is Cinderella's foot, of course. When he finds her, he marries her and they live happily ever after.

Character—A character is a person in a story.

Climax—In most stories all the action leads up to one very important event, which is often a turning point of some kind. This usually comes toward the end of the story, and it is called the climax. In long books there are often many small climaxes before the big climax. In some stories it's hard to pick out the climax at all because it might have more to do with a character's changing emotions than with something concrete.

Setting—Setting is where and when the action of a story takes place—the time and location. The setting might be "Morocco, 1942" or "Indianapolis, 1995" or "Sam Whittaker's garage, last Sunday night." So when someone asks you where a story is "set," she wants to know *where and when* the action happens.

Dialogue—In a story dialogue refers to the words spoken by the characters. Some authors rely heavily on dialogue because they like to let the characters' voices move the plot along.

Novel—A long piece of fiction. Novels are book-length stories.

Novella—A short novel. There is no set page length at which novellas become novels. If it's over a hundred pages, people will probably call it a novel, but that's only a general guideline.

Short story—A short piece of fiction. Short stories can be as short as one page or as long as forty pages—or even longer. Long short stories could be called novellas. There aren't any exact rules, but somewhere around forty pages, short stories are called novellas.

✎ ✎ ✎ ✎ ✎

"Okay, are you ready?" asked Zenobia. "Here we go . . ."

STEP 1: What's the big idea?

"It's pretty much common sense that before you start writing a story, you ought to have an idea. But deciding what to write isn't exactly like picking out clothes or choosing what to eat for lunch. You might try as hard as you can to think of a story idea one day and not come up with anything, but on another day you might have five or six great ideas. It's important to write down story ideas as soon as you get them, even if you don't write the story until months later."

"But I'm afraid my story ideas will never be as good as the idea for *Frankenstein*," sighed Barnaby.

"That's where you're wrong," replied Zenobia. "Who knows? You might write a great horror novel that becomes even more popular than *Frankenstein* some day, if that's what you decide to do. But story ideas don't have to be grand or dramatic or scary or heroic to be good. Many stories set in regular towns with regular people as characters are just as enduring and interesting—sometimes even *more* enduring and interesting because readers find more to identify with. They can see themselves and their lives in the story.

"Don't worry about whether everyone will like your story, because not everyone will. Stories are a matter of taste. All that matters is that *you* feel strongly about your story idea, okay?"

Barnaby nodded.

Zenobia smiled. "Since we are racing against the clock, I won't be able to spend months and months with you while you write your first novels. So this training will be in the format of the *short story*. With that in mind, give me your best ideas!"

✍ EXERCISE #11 ✍
Write Down Your Ideas

Write down ideas for three short stories. You
don't have to go into very much detail. Just
give the general idea for each one.

1. _____

_____

_____

_____

2. _____

_____

_____

_____

3. _____

_____

_____

_____

STEP 2: What's your purpose?

"Let's say you wrote this down as a story
idea.

A boy in a small Midwestern town has a regular
life. His mother stays home and takes care of
the house and the new baby, and his father
works all the time and always comes home tired
and watches television. They don't have much

money. One day the boy comes home from school early after a field trip, and hears music coming from his house. He looks in the window and sees his mother in a fancy dress he's never seen before, and she's dancing by herself in the living room. He watches for a while but doesn't go in. Instead, he goes for a long walk, and when he comes home again his mother is in her regular clothes and everything is normal.

"This will work as a story, but before you start writing it, ask yourself why you want to write it," Zenobia explained. "You have the basic events of the story, but what are they supposed to show? That the boy's mother is crazy? That she likes to dance around in fancy clothes? That the boy's father is boring? You have to decide what your purpose is.

"Don't think you have to come up with some kind of moral lesson. Your story doesn't have to prove anything. It's enough to paint a good picture or create an exact emotion. You just have to decide what you're trying to achieve before you start writing. Knowing your purpose helps you avoid getting sidetracked when you write.

"So for our story idea, let's state the purpose as

To show a boy realizing that his mother is a woman who feels bored and lonely, and that she longs for the romance and excitement she might have had when she was younger, or maybe that she missed out on.

"Do you see how that works as a purpose? If this story seems a little complicated, don't worry. Your purpose can be very simple and straightforward and still be deep, moving, and interesting.

"If you want to write a story about the day your best friend moved away, it's enough to say that your purpose is to show that losing a friend is painful and scary. If you want to write a story about rebel soldiers in outer space defeating an evil empire of aliens that use dark and wicked powers, it's enough to say your purpose is to show good triumphing over evil.

"When you first start writing stories, it's a good idea to start small and simple. Start with a purpose you know you can accomplish. As your writing skills improve, you can take on more difficult emotions and ideas," Zenobia advised.

"So, I suppose you want us to write down a purpose for each of our story ideas now," said Bridget, grinning.

"What a perceptive girl you are!" cried Zenobia. "Yes, that's exactly what I want you to do."

✍ **EXERCISE #12** ✍
A Sense of Purpose

For each of your story ideas in Exercise #11, write a clear statement of purpose.

1. _____

_____

_____

_____

2. _____

_____

_____

_____

3. _____

_____

_____

_____

STEP 3: Think it through

"Now you are almost ready to write, but before you do, take a little time to think the whole thing through, from start to finish."

_____

Think about your plot. How will the action in your story unfold? Think through the scenes in your story from start to finish. Who will be in them? Where will they take place?

Who are your characters? Decide who your characters are—and not just names and ages. What do they look like? What are their personalities? Does one character have a special walk or laugh? You should feel that you *know* the people you are writing about enough to answer any question about them. You should have a feel for the way they would speak, including the things they would and would not say.

Who tells the story? This is a very difficult decision for many storytellers. There are two main options, and both have advantages and disadvantages.

One option is called **first-person narration.** That is a fancy way of saying that one of the characters will tell the story. It will be told from the "I" point of view. Using a first-person narrator makes your story seem closer to the reader, but the problem is that you can only include things in the story if your narrator sees or feels them. Any description, any talk about what other characters are doing or feeling, has to come from the narrator. That can be hard to do, but many authors decide the difficulty is worthwhile.

The other option is called the **third person** point of view. Third person uses "he" or "she" instead of "I." These narrators are **omniscient,** which means that they see everything and know everything that is going on. However, the narrator is not a character and does not participate in the action.

As you read more you will come across variations on these options, and sometimes combinations. If you decide to experiment with point of view, be careful. Even experienced authors have trouble with this part of writing. Always be mindful of who your narrator is and what the limitations of the narrator are.

Set the pace. Has someone ever started telling you a joke but taken so long to get to the punchline that when he finally did, you just didn't care anymore? That's an example of a problem with pacing. Sometimes the punchline is such a knockout that it needs a good, long wind-up to get people ready for it. Other times, a joke would be a lot funnier if it got to the point more quickly.

It's the same with a story. A sense of pacing is one of the hardest things for an author to develop. Some authors take a long time to write a story, so they may *think* the pace is slow, but when they read over what they've written, they realize the action moves too quickly. Other authors get caught up writing long descriptions and scenes that don't really move the action along and later realize that their story is too bogged down.

Before you start writing, have a general idea of how long your story is going to be. Keep your purpose in mind and decide how much support that purpose needs from your scenes and characters. Read through what you write to make sure it flows the way you want.

"Once you've thought all that through—and it may take a whole day, or days, or even weeks—then you are ready to begin writing," concluded Zenobia. "Select one of your story ideas and go think it through. When you've finished, let me know."

STEP 4: Write your story

The safari had taken them quite a long way. The travelers had started out crossing grassy plains and now were traversing a desert so hot that the air seemed to waver just above the ground. There were no trees—only small sand dunes swelling like ocean waves. Barnaby, Babette, and Bridget had been thinking for a long time and scribbling notes on their pads. Beauregard, for all his fur, seemed the least affected by the heat. He just pulled his hat lower over his eyes and rode calmly on. Finally, one of the questers spoke.

"Zenobia, I'm ready. I've thought it all through and I want to start writing," said Bridget seriously. She pulled the top off her canteen and took a long swig of water.

"Are you now?" asked Zenobia. "And what about you two?"

"I think I am ready," said Babette. Barnaby nodded in agreement.

Zenobia paused and looked at them for a moment. "I have to warn you, you may think developing an idea is hard, but writing—the actual act of putting words together to tell a good story—is much more difficult. Especially from the back of a horse, crossing the largest desert in the world. Do you think you're up to it?"

Bridget, Barnaby, and Babette didn't even have to answer. Zenobia could tell from the determined looks on their faces that they had no intention of stopping now.

The safari leader let out a satisfied sigh. "All right, then. Let me give you some writing pointers."

FLESHING OUT FANTASIES

"Let me return to the question you asked a while back, Barnaby," Zenobia continued. "I was telling you that good writers use personal experiences when writing, and you asked if that meant that you couldn't make things up.

The answer is no, of course not. As a writer of fiction, you are free to make up anything you want. Let your imagination run wild! Make up crazy subterranean settings and strange alien creatures if you feel like it. But bear this in mind—*whatever you make up must seem believable.* That's where personal experience comes in very handy. Do you write your observations in journals?"

Barnaby, Bridget, and Babette all nodded.

"Good," said Zenobia. "Your journals are great sources of information. You've written down feelings, pieces of conversation, thoughts—your personal stockpile of raw story material. Do with it as you choose. If you thought part of a conversation you heard was funny or interesting, use it in a story. If you think your school's principal is a wicked, hateful person, use his personality to create a villain in a story. You can even piece together different parts of different people you know to create a character. All the things you feel and see can be included, and the more you use from your own experience, the *truer* your fiction will be."

"I thought fiction wasn't supposed to be true," said Bridget.

"You're right, it isn't true, in the sense that it isn't factual. But it should *seem* true, even if it's a story about three-legged monsters on the planet Zoltag," explained Zenobia. "Think of your life as a kitchen full of baking supplies or a workshop full of wood and paint and tools. Your life has given you the supplies, and you can use them to bake or build whatever you want—even something that's never existed before."

Beauregard says you can learn a lot from empathy. Your personal experiences are going to be limited by the fact that you are only one person. You see things through your own eyes. But, as the old saying goes, you'll never understand another person until you've walked a mile in her shoes. "Empathy" means putting yourself in someone else's shoes and feeling what she feels. Feeling empathy is not only a great way to get story ideas and strengthen your writing, it also makes you a more understanding person.

Try it out on one of your parents if you want. You're used to them and the way they act with you, but try feeling what your mother or father feels—and look at them as just people, not your parents. Pretend you have to work and pay bills and shop for groceries and take care of children. How does it feel? What do you think makes your parents laugh? What kind of kids do you think they were? How do other adults react to them? What's it like to have you as a son or daughter?

Details, Details: Making Your Reader See What You See

"To make readers see and hear and feel something as if it were real, you have to describe it well. If you are using personal experience, that makes it easy—you actually *did* see or feel what you are writing about. But if you are creating something from your imagination, you have to be careful not to be *shallow*. It's your responsibility to breathe life into your creations," warned Zenobia.

"What does *shallow* mean?" asked Bridget. "I know what shallow water is, but how can a story be shallow?"

"*Shallow* means thin, flimsy, not fleshed out—like a cardboard cutout of a person instead of flesh and blood," Zenobia said. "If the people and places in your story are shallow, the story won't be very interesting. Characters can be shallow, and so can the setting, the action, and the dialogue, if they don't bring the story to life for the reader."

"How can we keep from being shallow?" asked Barnaby, his forehead wrinkling with concern. "I don't want to be boring."

"The answer is in the *details*," replied Zenobia. "Remember Step 3? Before you start writing, you have to think through the details of your plot, setting, and characters. But it's easy to forget to give those details to the reader. As the author you already have a picture in your head of what you are describing, but your reader doesn't have that benefit.

"Some authors like to give descriptions all at once. For instance, each time a new character is introduced, they tell you everything about him or her. That works sometimes, but sometimes it interrupts the flow of a story. Other authors like to reveal their characters more slowly, so they give details as the story progresses. The same goes for setting. You have to decide what works best in each story you write."

Zenobia paused in thought for a second. "You know, it is so important to flesh out your stories with details that I think we should do another exercise."

Beauregard says details make the scene. Notice how John Kennedy Toole uses detailed description to make you see the scene in the following passage from *The Neon Bible:*

Tonight wasn't like the night before when it had been so still in the valley. A breeze was starting that soon turned into a wind. It was nice to sit on the steps and watch the pines on the far hills swaying against the sky. I looked around at Aunt Mae. Her yellow hair was flying all over her eyes, but she didn't move to straighten it. Her eyes were on the town, I don't know exactly what part. They were just staring down on the town.

It got dark on the porch after the clouds began to cover the moon. Pretty soon there was just a white glow in the sky covered by gray smoke. You could see the shadows of the clouds on the hills moving fast across the valley. Soon the whole sky was full of gray smoke from the south, and it looked like the valley had a gray lid on it. A rumbling began at the far hill and spread across the sky until it shook the house. The sky lit up off and on like one of the signs on Main Street, except without color, just a silver glow. The kind of cool breeze that always comes before a rain started up, and soon I could hear the first big drops on the porch roof and feel them hitting my knees. They hit the clay with a steady thump and made the cinders shine.

✍ EXERCISE #13 ✍
Give Me the Details

Below is a list of people, things, and places, accompanied by some questions. Use your imagination to come up with a specific example of the general concept and then answer the questions in as much detail as possible.

1. A famous painter

    What does he or she look like (height, hair, eyes, face)?

    _____

    _____

    _____

    What kind of clothes does the painter wear?

    _____

    _____

    _____

    What kind of food does the painter eat?

    _____

    _____

    _____

    What is the painter's favorite song?

    _____

    _____

    _____

    What are the painter's habits?

    _____

    _____

    _____

2. An alien creature from a distant planet

How does the creature move from place to place?

_____

_____

_____

What does the creature look like?

_____

_____

_____

What does the creature eat?

_____

_____

_____

What does the creature do for fun?

_____

_____

_____

How would you talk to it?

_____

_____

_____

3. A royal palace

    In what part of the world is the palace?

    _____

    _____

    _____

    When was it built?

    _____

    _____

    _____

    From what material is the palace constructed?

    _____

    _____

    _____

    How many rooms does the palace have?

    _____

    _____

    _____

    Who lives in the palace?

    _____

    _____

    _____

What is the most beautiful thing in the palace?

_____

_____

_____

4. The person you will marry some day

What does he or she look like?

_____

_____

_____

What makes the person laugh?

_____

_____

_____

Where does the person come from?

_____

_____

_____

What kind of job does the person have?

_____

_____

_____

How did you fall in love with the person?

_____

_____

_____

5. A wizard's house

In what part of the world is the wizard's house?

_____

_____

_____

What kind of furniture does the wizard have?

_____

_____

_____

What's on the wizard's shelves?

_____

_____

_____

What's the most dangerous thing in the house?

_____

_____

_____

※ ※ ※ ※ ※

"I hope that's worked any kinks out of your descriptive abilities," said Zenobia. "But before you begin writing, I have a few last words of advice."

SHOW, DON'T TELL

"People like to feel they're *in* a story, or witnessing a story," she explained, taking off her hat and wiping some sweat off her forehead with the back of her sleeve. "Don't insult your readers by telling them what emotions to have or what to pay attention to. If you paint your scenes and characters well, they will see what you want them to without you beating them over the head. This is called showing instead of telling, and I suppose I should give you some examples.

Telling—When Frederick saw Kathy so pale and still in the hospital bed, he felt sad and scared and all torn up inside. He didn't know what to do with himself, so he hung around awhile, and then left.

Showing—When Frederick saw Kathy so pale and still in the hospital bed, he stopped and stood very still, unaware of the tears in his eyes until they began trickling down his face. When he reached up his hand to wipe them away, he noticed that his fists were clenched tightly.

Frederick took a deep breath, relaxed his hands, and lit up a cigarette, but he put it out right away. He looked absently through the old, wrinkled magazines on the table in the hall. He got up and stared out the dark window, watching his breath fog up the glass. Then he turned and walked quickly out into the rainy night.

Telling—Rhonda waited for her mother to pick her up from school. Rhonda had just had the best day of her whole life, and she couldn't wait to talk about it.

Showing—Rhonda stood outside the main entrance of the school building, dancing around on her tip toes and peering down the street, looking for her mother's car. She was singing to herself, and she was grinning like a fool, but she didn't care one bit if anyone noticed.

When she finally saw her mother's tan Lincoln pulling into the parking lot, she half ran, half skipped out to meet her.

✎ ✎ ✎ ✎ ✎

"Do you see the difference between showing and telling?" asked Zenobia.

"I think so," said Barnaby. "But don't you have to tell some things? Won't people get confused otherwise?"

"You'll have to explain a lot less than you think if you stick to your purpose and give good descriptions. Before you go off explaining or 'telling' something, try to think of a way you could *show* it instead. Your story will be better for it," answered the safari leader.

"Are we ready? Can we start writing now?" asked Bridget eagerly.

"Hmm, well, I suppose you should know one important Rule first. . . ." mused Zenobia.

"Oh, boy, here comes another Rule!" cried Barnaby.

"And that rule is . . ."

RULE #5
Write like yourself.

"You know, the weird thing about these Rules we keep learning is that I never understand them," sighed Barnaby, shaking his head.

"Come now, Barnaby," said Zenobia. "The Rule is simple enough. Basically, 'write like yourself' means you should develop your own style and be comfortable with it."

"I get it!" said Bridget. "It's kind of like when my mother tells me the best way to make friends is to relax and be myself instead of putting on some kind of act. She says every person has a unique personality and he or she should let it shine through."

Zenobia nodded. "That's right. But a writer's personality is called a **voice** or **style**. And styles can be as different as personalities. Some writers' voices are like fireworks crashing and banging and blazing through the night and other voices are like flowers slowly blooming."

"Pardon me?" asked a confused Babette.

"Sorry. There I go rambling again. What I mean is there are as many different styles as there are writers, and none is necessarily better than another," she continued. "It can take a lot of trial and error for you to discover what *your* voice is, but once you figure it out, be proud of it. Don't feel you have to write like someone else.

"When you first start writing, you might find you naturally copy the styles of the writers you like the most. That's okay for a beginner, but don't be satisfied with it. Keep trying to write like yourself."

Babette, Barnaby, and Bridget nodded and looked expectantly at their safari leader. She had an unreadable smile on her tough face as she issued her order.

"Well, that's it, kids. What are you waiting for? Start writing!"

Beauregard says writing is a matter of personal style. Writing styles are as diverse as people. Compare the following two passages. Both are about a young man traveling alone, yet they differ greatly. The first passage is from *Jacob's Room* by Virginia Woolf, a British writer from the 1920s. The second passage is from *On the Road* by Jack Kerouac, an American writer from the 1950s.

Jacob heard them crying strange names at railway stations through the night. The train stopped and he heard frogs croaking close by, and he wrinkled back the blind cautiously and saw a vast strange marsh all white in the moonlight. The carriage was thick with cigar smoke, which floated round the globe with the green shade on it. The Italian gentleman lay snoring with his boots off and his waistcoat unbuttoned. . . . And all this business of going to Greece seemed to Jacob an intolerable weariness—sitting in hotels by oneself and looking at monuments—he'd have done better to go to Cornwall with Timmy Durrant. . . .

from *Jacob's Room*, Virginia Woolf

The greatest ride in my life was about to come up, a truck, with a flatboard at the back, with about six or seven boys sprawled out on it, and the drivers, two young blond farmers from Minnesota, were picking up every single soul they found on that road—the most smiling, cheerful couple of handsome bumpkins you could ever wish to see, both wearing cotton shirts and overalls, nothing else; both thick-wristed and earnest, with broad howareyou smiles for anybody and anything that came across their path. I ran up, said "Is there room?" They said, "Sure, hop on, 'sroom for everybody."

from *On the Road*, Jack Kerouac

The sun was slowly sinking ahead of them, and their shadows began to lengthen. No one knew for sure how long they had been riding along in silence. The terrain they traveled gradually turned from desert into plains into desert.

A long time after they had exhausted their water supply, the weary travelers stopped at a small watering hole beside a hill to refresh themselves and their animals and to rest.

"Ummphh," groaned Barnaby, sinking to the ground against a palm tree and pouring water from his newly filled canteen over his head.

Bridget and Babette were splashing water on their faces at the spring. Zenobia and Beauregard seemed to be having a quiet discussion several yards away.

"So, did you finish?" Bridget asked Babette.

Babette nodded, smiling. Her face was sunburned and her lips chapped, but she looked happy. Bridget smiled back.

"Hey, Barnaby!" she called to her reclining friend. "How did it go?"

"I think I'm officially a writer," Barnaby said. "Actually, next to taking a bath and sleeping for twelve hours, writing another story is the thing I want to do most right now."

"Well, you're in luck then," said Zenobia. "You have finished your quest. It is time for you to return to Paris. I have to go back the way I came. I'll have to take the horses with me, I'm afraid."

Barnaby pushed himself up off the ground. Bridget and Babette turned and looked at her in disbelief.

"But Zenobia, we're in the middle of a desert! We have no idea where we are!" cried Babette.

"It's not my fault you kids don't study geography," quipped the safari leader.

"How do we get back to Paris?" asked Bridget.

"What do I look like, Glinda the Good Witch of the North? You'll have to figure that out on your own. I don't see any ruby slippers on any of you, so I guess you can't click your heels and say 'There's no place like Paris.' But I will give you a hint: Remember how you left, and you'll learn how to return."

"Zenobia, please don't leave us!" begged Barnaby, but she was already on her horse and was busy gathering in the others.

"Oh, quit whining," she said. "Why don't you all go to the top of that hill? I'm sure the view will make you feel a lot better."

And with that she shook paws with Beauregard, waved to the questers, and rode off.

"Great, that's just great!" yelled Barnaby, kicking the sand. "We're all going to die!"

"Barnaby, throwing a tantrum isn't going to help us," sighed Babette. "We might as well climb the hill. Look—Beauregard is halfway up it already."

Sure enough, Beauregard was well ahead of them. And he had turned to wait for them to follow.

Chapter 10

Downstairs, Upstairs, and Online

I tell you, sometimes taking those kids and dragging them by the earlobes seems like a good idea. They should know by now that they are neither helpless nor defenseless. Bridget could have blown one of those balloons of hers, and we would have been out of there in a jiffy. But if I hadn't taken some action and gotten them to follow me, they probably would have sat around bellyaching for hours.

There was no need for all their fussing. Zenobia didn't leave them stranded, she was just pulling their legs. Once they climbed to the top of the hill after me, they could see that we were only about a mile away from a large city, and beyond the city was a glimmering ocean. I could tell Bridget and Babette were delighted to be so close to civilization. Barnaby was also relieved but a little ticked off about the joke Zenobia had played on them.

We ran back down the hill so the kids could gather their stuff and then set off on foot for the oceanfront town. While I was saying good-bye to Zenobia, I tried to get her to tell me how to get back to Paris quickly, but she just smiled that mysterious smile of hers and made a joke about how I had no business hooking up with a bunch of young questers if I didn't have the energy for it. Ah, well, I guess she's right. It's their quest, and they'll have to figure it out. What was it she said to Barnaby? Something like, "Remember how you left Paris, and you'll learn how to return."

✎ ✎ ✎ ✎ ✎

The townsfolk were mostly dressed in loose, cotton robes and seemed too busy going and coming and talking to each other to notice the dusty strangers following a gigantic black cat into town. Once they reached a stone fountain in what appeared to be the central square, Beauregard decided to stop leading the way. He just sat down and waited.

"Well, here we are," said Bridget matter-of-factly.

"What do you mean, 'here we are'?" demanded Barnaby, who obviously had not recovered from his irritation with Zenobia. "We have no idea where we are!"

"On the contrary," said Babette. "Listen—the people are speaking French."

Barnaby listened. "But surely we're not in France!" he protested.

"No, of course not," said Babette. "We are in Morocco; the city of Casablanca, to be exact. It used to be French territory."

"How do you know we're in Casablanca?" asked Bridget.

"Because the sign over there says 'Café Casablanca,'" answered Babette, pointing to a whitewashed building across the square.

"Say, you don't suppose they'd let us use their restrooms, do you?" asked Barnaby. "I mean, we can't buy anything to eat, but I sure would like to use a little soap and water."

"I don't think it should be a problem," said Babette. "We just have to be cool. Let's go."

Bridget, Babette, Barnaby, and Beauregard crossed the square and walked into the Café Casablanca as casually as possible. They paused to look at the menu, pretending that they intended to order something, and then walked calmly toward the back of the room. In a little hallway there were three doors marked in Arabic script. Barnaby reached for the

center door and was about to open it when Babette grabbed his arm.

"That door is marked 'cellar,' Barnaby," she said. "The one on the left is the men's room."

"You read Arabic?" asked Bridget

"Of course," replied Babette. "Enough to get around with, anyway."

"Hey, wait a minute you two," began Barnaby, who had not taken his hand off the door handle. "Didn't Zenobia say we could get back to Paris by remembering how we left?"

"Yes, she did. Not very good directions, if you ask me," said Bridget. "At least we know we need to go north. I hope I have enough energy to blow a bubble."

"If what I'm thinking is right, you won't have to!" Barnaby cried. "Zenobia said to remember how we left Paris. We left Paris by going into a cellar. When we left the cellar, we were someplace else. Do you think if we go into this cellar, we'll come back out in Paris?"

"I think the sun has fried your brain," snapped Bridget.

"Oh, so you think it's silly, huh?" he retorted. "Well, what I'm suggesting doesn't seem so weird when you compare it to the other things that have happened to us."

"What do you suggest, Barnaby?" asked Babette soothingly. "That we just go into the cellar and then come out?"

"Exactly! What do we have to lose? If it doesn't work, Bridget can blow a bubble."

"I guess it couldn't hurt," agreed Bridget.

"Fine, then," said Babette. "Barnaby, lead the way."

Barnaby opened the cellar door wide. Beyond the door was complete darkness. He felt around the wall for a light switch but found none, so he slowly eased himself into the blackness. One by one, Bridget, Babette, and Beauregard followed him, and when the last of Beauregard's tail was inside, a sudden breeze slammed the door shut behind them.

"Yipes!" cried Bridget. "I hate loud noises."

"Can you feel the stairs?" asked Barnaby. "Let's go down so we have more room."

Slowly, they walked down, down, down, carefully feeling ahead of them with their hands and feet. The cellar steps seemed endless. Finally, Babette stopped.

"Barnaby, I mean no offense to your idea, but after further consideration, I do not think we should proceed," she said, trying to control her nervousness. "A bottomless cellar in Casablanca is not where I think we should end our quest."

Barnaby sighed in the darkness. "I think you're right. Sorry about this. Let's go back up."

With Beauregard leading the way, the questers inched their way back up the stairs. It seemed to be taking even longer than coming down. The procession halted abruptly when Babette bumped into a furry backside.

"Oooh! Excuse me, Beauregard. Have you reached the door?" she asked.

She was answered with a scratching that could only have been Beauregard's claws on wood. And, to her great relief, his clawing was followed by the sight of a thin, dim strip of light as the door swung slightly open.

"Whew!" sighed Bridget. "Thanks, Beauregard. Go on out, okay?"

The door opened wide to reveal . . . the Mute Café in Paris!

"Oh my goodness, I really don't believe this!" gasped Bridget.

"Um, yes, well, you see I thought as much," said Barnaby, equally surprised, but obviously proud of himself. Babette had already followed Beauregard into the main room.

Their happiness and relief was quickly replaced by concern, however. Rain was pouring down in the darkness outside the café. When a flash of lightning streaked across the sky, they could see flood waters rising as high as the windows. The waiter rushed toward them, his eyes wild and hopeful.

"You have returned at last—just when I had given up hope!" he cried, his voice mingling with the sound of thunder. "Did you succeed? Have you learned the five Rules of Good Writing? Quickly, say the Rules before it's too late!"

"Take it easy, man, I have them here somewhere mixed in with my other stuff," said Bridget, flipping through her notebook.

"Don't worry, I wrote them all on one page," said Barnaby. "Now, where is that page . . ."

"Quickly, we haven't much time!" urged the waiter.

"I believe I remember them," said Babette.

RULE #1
Rules are made to be broken— but only on purpose.

RULE #2
Clear writing demands clear thinking.

RULE #3
Know your audience.

RULE #4
Writers write or, in other words, writers who do not write are not writers.

RULE #5
Write like yourself.

With the last word Babette pronounced, the waiter leaned back, threw his arms above his head, and let out a deafening "Ahhhhhhhhhhhhhhhhhh!" Babette shrank away from him and huddled together with Bridget, Barnaby, and Beauregard. Then the waiter started hopping wildly around the room shouting "Yes, Yes, Yes!" and finally ended his prancing over by the window. He stared out at the street with what appeared to be great contentment. The questers eyed him warily.

"Come over here, kids. Take a look at what you have done," he said, beckoning to them.

He seemed to have regained his senses, so they walked over to him and peered cautiously out the window.

The rain had stopped completely, and the flood waters were steadily receding. As the minutes passed the sky took on a pale gray light, which soon turned to the reddish gold of a beautiful sunrise.

Bridget sighed happily and was turning to say something to her friends when she saw a movement out of the corner of her eye. She spun around to see what was there, and her jaw dropped in amazement: Hedda and Frizzy from the old western town stood arm in arm. Captain Lucid was leaning against the bar next to Mr. Dexter Fairley. Peeper Airborne was pulling off her cap and shaking out her shining, red curls. Ikiko was stroking his white mustache thoughtfully. And Zenobia, towering over them all, stood with her powerful hands on her hips and a wide grin on her face.

Bridget was so shocked that she couldn't speak.

"Henri!" barked Zenobia. "After a quest like that, these kids deserve some breakfast, wouldn't you agree?"

The waiter, whose name must have been Henri, turned around, as did Babette and Barnaby, and smiles and hugs and handshakes were exchanged all around. Henri enlisted Hedda's aid in the kitchen, and soon questers and guides alike were sitting down to a hearty French breakfast of cheese and eggs and crusty bread. The clattering of utensils and the happy chatter of writers filled the air. Beauregard sat next to Zenobia, eating a plate of sardines.

Halfway through the meal, Bridget almost choked when Henri reminded her that she and her friends had left an unpaid bill.

"I trust you have returned with something to pay for those drinks you ordered, young lady. Remember, I only accept writing in exchange for my services," he demanded with a little smile.

Bridget stared at him for a moment and then reached for her notebook. She handed it to him across the table, and he carefully began turning the pages and nodding to himself, occasionally muttering something. After several agonizing minutes, he finally spoke.

"Yes, this will more than take care of the bill. I am honored to have such a fine young *writer* at my table," he said.

Bridget blushed with pleasure at the way he emphasized "writer."

"Come, Bridget, Babette, Barnaby. Now that you have completed your quest, there are a couple of matters I would like to discuss with you."

COMPUTERS: A WRITER'S BEST FRIEND

Henri gathered the questers together at a table by the window. On the table was some sort of boxy object covered by a tasseled purple scarf.

"I see you all have been very carefully writing in your notebooks," said Henri. "That is wonderful. It is always important for a writer to have something to write *on* whenever the mood strikes. But let me ask you something—didn't you find it difficult to make changes and move things around in your reports and stories? Writing everything out is so time-consuming, don't you think?"

Babette agreed. "I always go back and see things I want to do differently, so I have to mark things up or start again. It is bothersome."

"Well, we have at least one thing to be grateful for living in this day and age, and that is computers!" cried Henri, whisking the purple scarf away to reveal a well-stocked personal computer with a big color screen.

"Wow," said Barnaby. "Nice screen."

"Yes, the screen is nice, but that's not what's important. Almost any personal computer will help you immeasurably in your writing. If you have a computer at home, you're very lucky. You shouldn't waste such a valuable resource. Use it.

"If you don't have a computer at home, you may have access to one at your school. Many high schools and junior high schools are equipped with computer labs that students can use to write reports and papers."

Henri leaned toward them to emphasize his point. "Most colleges have some sort of computer facility students can use—some even provide students with computers—so it's important for you to learn to use this tool. If your school doesn't have computers, ask your teachers and parents to help you track down a computer you can spend some time on."

Barnaby, Bridget, and Babette nodded to show that they understood.

"Good," said Henri. "You're probably wondering why computers are so great for writing. One reason is the rise of *word-processing programs*."

The Wonders of Word Processing

"Most personal computers come equipped with a word-processing program—*a package of software specifically designed for the task of writing*," explained Henri. "Many of the programs are 'user friendly,' which is a computer term that means 'easy to use.' You could start the morning having no idea how to operate the program and, with a little instruction, be a master of the program by lunchtime."

"I'm glad to know that using word-processing programs is so easy," said Bridget. "But what makes using a computer any better than using a typewriter or writing on paper?"

"The capabilities of computers are vastly superior to those of typewriters," sniffed Henri. "It's like comparing rollerskates to an all-terrain truck. The following are just a few of the things word-processing programs can do for you."

Correct your spelling. You can use a "spell check" function to search through your document for misspelled words. Word processors have built-in dictionaries that look up every single word for you. These spell checkers are so good that they can usually figure out what word you were trying to type even if you spelled it completely wrong.

That doesn't mean you don't have to look over what you write, though. For instance, if your document says "his is outrageous" when you meant to say "this is outrageous," the spell checker won't catch the mistake because "his" is spelled correctly.

Make your documents neater. When you type something on a typewriter, you have to do a lot of figuring. You have to set the margins and decide when to return at the end of every line. If you want to center something in the middle of the page, you may have to do a couple of mathematical equations to figure out how to place it. It can be even worse if you write things out by hand. If you mess up, you have to use white correction fluid, and that can leave an even bigger mess.

Computers do the figuring for you. Standard margins are already set. You just clatter away on the keyboard, and the program decides when to shift to the next line. If you want to center something, all it takes is the click of a button. And if you make a mistake, you can just go back and fix it and the computer makes the necessary adjustments to the rest of your paper. The result is one handsome document!

Do global searches and replacements. Say you're writing a story that takes place in Iceland, and you're almost done when you think to yourself, "You know, this would be much more interesting if it were set in Mongolia." If you were writing your story by hand, you'd probably smack yourself in the forehead at that point because you'd have to go back to the beginning and find every place in which you wrote "Iceland," cross it out, and write "Mongolia" instead. And what if you miss a couple of places where you wrote "Iceland"? That would make your story rather confusing, wouldn't it?

Ah, but a computer saves you the trouble! It can search for every occurence of the word "Iceland" and replace each one with "Mongolia" all at once. This same function also makes it possible to search for a word or words. For example, say you are writing an explanatory note to your father about how a certain window happened to get smashed by a baseball. You've gone on spouting all sorts of different theories, but after about twenty pages, you can't remember if you've mentioned your hailstorm theory yet. Instead of rereading all twenty pages of the note, you can just search for "hailstorm" and see if the name of the theory appears in the note. Aren't computers great?

Make notes to yourself. Writing a paper or a story can be a difficult task that drags on for days, and sometimes you can get stuck on certain parts. Maybe you want to use a quote from a magazine article you read, but you don't have the article with you. If you're writing by hand, what do you do? You can leave a blank space and go back to it later, but how do you know how much space you'll need? Or you could just stop until you get the article, but that could cost you a lot of time. If you're writing on a computer, though, you can make yourself a note like "PUT QUOTE FROM *NATIONAL GEOGRAPHIC* MONKEY ARTICLE HERE," and then go on with the rest of your paper. You then can go back to your note when you have the material you need. All kinds of reminders or suggestions to yourself can be sprinkled throughout your paper.

If you like to have other people read through your work, they can also leave you notes and comments this way. If you don't like what they have to say, you can just delete their suggestions.

Add, replace, and reorder text. There is a "cut and paste" function in most word-processing programs that is a dream come true for writers. After writing a story or paper, an author might decide that the sequence of scenes is all wrong. If the author were writing by hand or typing, she would have to throw her whole draft away. But the cut-and-paste function saves a lot of trouble. It allows you to mark a block of text that you want to put elsewhere, cut it, and move it in a matter of seconds. You can move several paragraphs or just one phrase, and not have to retype a thing.

The same function allows you to replace pieces of your document. For example, say you've been working on several versions of a story and the ending is giving you trouble. Finally, after the seventh attempt, you like the story, but you decide you like your second version of the ending best. If you saved that version (more on this in a minute), all you have to do is highlight it, use the "copy" command to make a copy of it, and then "paste" it over the existing ending.

Save everything. For creative writers, the computer's ability to store documents is a great boon. Different versions of poems and stories can be stored while you figure out exactly which one you like best. Unfinished drafts can sit and wait for your next burst of inspiration. Of course, you can save your handwritten documents, but on a computer they don't clutter up your room and they can be easily changed and revised when you want to work on them again.

✎　✎　✎　✎　✎

"I could go on and on about the wonders of computers and word-processing programs," sighed Henri. "Believe me, there are many more benefits than the few I've just mentioned. Of course, one important skill you need to learn in order to get the most out of computers is **typing.**"

"You mean with both hands?" asked Barnaby.

Henri chuckled. "Yes, both hands. Learn to type quickly and accurately, and it will help you immeasurably, in your writing, in school, and on the job. You can learn to type much faster than you can print. If you get really good at it, you can type as fast as you can talk. I myself sometimes type faster than I think."

Babette narrowed her eyes at him and wondered if he was joking.

"At any rate," he continued without missing a beat, "if there is a typing class at your school, you might want to consider signing up for it. If not, there are plenty of books that can help you teach yourself. If you have a computer, you can even buy a software package that teaches you to type. The sooner you learn, the better.

"Now we're going to get into something even more exciting, as if word processing wasn't exciting enough. Computers are wondrous things, and we've barely scratched the surface of what they can do for you."

Welcome to the Internet

"Chances are that you've heard of the worldwide computer network known as the Internet," began Henri. "If you haven't become familiar with it yet, you can rest assured that you'll have some contact with it eventually. Once you realize what it can do for you, I can guarantee that you will not be able to get enough of it.

"Explaining something like the Internet can get complicated, so I'm going to break it down to make it as simple as possible. Be patient now—you'll see how this affects you soon enough."

What Is a Network?

A network is a bunch of computers that can "talk" to each other. They can share files, and the people who use them can send notes to each other. A network can be small and include only the computers at one office or school. A network can also be large, connecting many schools and businesses over wide spaces.

The Internet is a network of thousands and thousands of smaller networks that spans the entire globe. If someone in a small town in Germany, for instance, wants to use his computer to look up information on the New York Stock Exchange, he can, because the New York Stock Exchange network is part of the Internet. If a student in New Mexico wants to look up the latest Supreme Court decisions, she can, because they are posted on the Internet.

How Do Computers "Talk"?

They call each other up on the telephone, just like you and me. Seriously, they do! Computers in an office network are hooked together with cables, but computers in different parts of the country or world communicate with each other over telephone lines.

Of course, they speak computer language, which is digital, which means it uses pulsed signals instead of words. A device called a **modem** translates the words, numbers, and other information in a document into computer language. Modems can also translate computer language back into words and numbers. So if you are sitting at a computer in Philadelphia and you want to send a note to someone in Sacramento, your modem will put your note in computer language and send it across the phone lines to your friend. Your friend's modem will receive the note in computer language and translate it so he can read it on his computer screen.

What Is E-Mail?

E-mail is electronic mail: The notes you send from one computer to another are sent through e-mail. The great thing about e-mail is that it's so fast. A message you want to send to a friend across the country could arrive there in minutes instead of the days it would take by normal mail because it is traveling across a phone line instead of over land. If you have access to the Internet, you can e-mail anyone else on the Internet.

Okay, How Do I Get Access to the Internet?

Glad you asked. First of all, you must have a computer and a modem. Once you do, there are a couple of ways to get on the Internet. One way is to subscribe to an **online service** ("online" means hooked up to a network). Some of these services charge monthly fees, but they are usually not expensive.

You don't have to use an online service, however. With the right software, you can hook yourself up directly to the Internet. You local bookstore will have plenty of books that take you through the whole process.

The good thing about hooking yourself up is that you don't have to pay a fee. Most of the information on the Internet is available free of charge. The problem is that the Internet is so huge, it's easy to get lost in it. There's just so much information available that you don't know where to begin. You need to know what you're looking for before you start looking, which is difficult sometimes. Online services make it easier to find the information you need.

How Can I Find My Way Around the Internet?

The best way to navigate the Internet to find what you're looking for is to use a search engine. Some of the most popular and useful search engines are Yahoo!, Google, Excite, and Ask Jeeves. All you have to do is go to the search engine's website, type in your topic, and then search for it. The search engine will show you a list of websites that contain information about the topic you searched for. Some of these websites will be more useful than others, so you'll have to look through them to figure out which ones contain the information you want.

Why Should Writers Care About This Stuff?

Imagine having access to libraries full of information in the privacy of your own home. That's what the Internet offers you. For students writing research papers, that means trips to the library might not be necessary. Fiction writers can also look up facts and information to help them flesh out their stories. Remember that story about Mongolia we mentioned earlier? What if you needed to know what rivers are in that country, or what the food staples are, or even what some common names of Mongolian people are? You could use the Internet to find out.

✎ ✎ ✎ ✎ ✎

Barnaby, Babette, and Bridget stared at Henri with awe, visions of searching the Internet dancing in their heads. By the time he finished talking, it was well into mid-morning. Through the window they could see people bustling in the streets that had been empty when they first came to the café. That seemed so long ago now! Many of the people began filing in, looking for a place to sit. And, Babette was quick to notice, several of them had little notepads in their pockets.

Henri smiled at the questers and stood up. "Go ahead, enjoy yourself on the computer for a while," he said. "Practice your writing skills. I'll bring you some orange juice in a minute."

He turned and walked toward the new customers, spreading his arms wide. "Come in, please, come in. Have a seat," he said. "Welcome to the Muse Café."

As I said in the beginning, Barnaby, Babette, and Bridget certainly have a way of getting themselves into trouble. I'm sure you see what I mean by now. I've a good mind to let them fall flat on their faces next time they get some fool notion about taking off on an adventure. But I guess they did achieve something great this time. Writing is a skill and an art to be valued, after all.

The café filled up very quickly, and the kids seemed so involved with their writing that I decided not

to fight my way over to them to say goodbye. I'm not much on goodbyes anyway. Too sappy. No, sometimes it's best to head out the door while no one's looking, which is what I did.

But even as I strolled down the street, the Muse Café disappearing in the distance behind me, I got this sneaking suspicion that I'd be seeing them again a lot sooner than I expected. I guess I'd better get some rest.

Chapter 11

Writing Opportunities for Young Authors

Hello there, it's me, Beauregard, again. I'm glad you stuck around because there a few things I thought of that you might find useful. After learning all those fine writing skills, maybe you're thinking to yourself, "That's just dandy. Here I have all these writing ideas and nothing to do with them!" Well, never fear. I've come up with a list of outlets for your creative energies.

WRITING YOU CAN DO AT SCHOOL

The school newspaper or magazine—Most high schools and some junior high schools publish periodicals written and organized by students. Some schools have weekly or biweekly newspapers. Others have magazines that come out once or twice a year that accept all sorts of writing.

If you're not sure if your school has any such publication, ask your English teacher. You might even be able to join the staff. Working on a publication at school can be a lot of fun and it can teach you some valuable job skills—like cooperation and time management—that will help you later in life.

The yearbook—A good yearbook is much more than a bunch of student pictures. It is a record of an entire year. A lot of writing goes into a yearbook, and it takes a lot of work and creativity to put one together. Ask your English teacher how you can become part of the yearbook staff.

PUBLISHING YOUR WORK

Rules for submission to the following publications vary, so contact them for specific information. Remember that these listings are only the tip of the iceberg: many regular magazines and newspapers publish submissions from young writers from time to time, so don't be afraid to submit your work to any publication that interests you.

When you send something to a magazine or publisher, always send a brief business letter with your submission. The letter should explain who you are (age, name of school, grade) and why you are writing. Turn back to chapter 3 if you need pointers on letter writing.

The Acorn

1530 Seventh Street

Rock Island, IL 61201

This magazine is for kids from kindergarten through twelfth grade, and accepts all kinds of writing: poetry, articles, fiction, and nonfiction.

Boodle: By Kids, For Kids

P.O. Box 1049

Portland, IN 47371

(219) 726-8141

The audience for *Boodle* is kids up to age twelve. The whole magazine is made up of children's writing: poems, stories, articles, and even illustrations.

Calliope

30 Grove Street, Suite C

Peterborough, NH 03458

Calliope is a world history magazine for young people, and each issue focuses on a different idea, event, or theme. They accept short poems and some articles from kids, as long as they relate to the theme. Write them and find out what they have planned!

Children's Digest

1100 Waterway Blvd.

P.O. Box 567

Indianapolis, IN 46202

This mainly health-related magazine accepts fiction, nonfiction, and poetry from children up to age thirteen.

Creative Kids

Prufrock Press

P.O. Box 8813

Waco, TX 76714

If you're aged five to eighteen, this magazine will consider your submission of almost anything creative: poems, stories, music, art, and games.

Flying Pencil Press

P.O. Box 7667

Elgin, IL 60121

Fiction, nonfiction, and poems from children up to age fourteen are published in a paperback anthology.

Kopper Bear Press

P.O. Box 19454

Boulder, CO 80308

This is a book publisher for kids aged thirteen to twenty-one. Novels, short stories, nonfiction, and poems are accepted.

The McGuffey Writer

5128 Westgate Drive

Oxford, OH 45056

Short stories, poems, songs, and nonfiction are accepted by this magazine devoted to children's writing. Anyone in kindergarten through high school is welcome to submit.

Merlyn's Pen: Fiction, Essays, & Poems by America's Teens

P.O. Box 910

East Greenwich, RI 02818

Practically any kind of writing from students in grades seven through ten is accepted by this magazine: essay, plays, reviews, poems, stories—even puzzles.

Stone Soup, The Magazine by Children

Children's Art Foundation

P.O. Box 83

Santa Cruz, CA 95063

(800) 447-4569

Authors published in this magazine actually get paid ($20 to $35) for their poems, illustrations, and stories. Submissions from students up to age thirteen are welcomed.

Whole Notes

P.O. Box 1374

Las Cruces, NM 88004

(505) 541-5744

Whole Notes publishes all sorts of poetry and has special editions for the works of young people up to age twenty-one. All poetry forms are considered.

WRITING CONTESTS

These are only a few of the hundreds of writing contests open to young people. Contests and competitions are often sponsored or administered by schools, newspapers, magazines, or businesses, so keep your eyes open. Many of them offer large cash prizes and scholarships.

Rules for entering each contest change often, so be sure to write for the most current information.

Delacorte Press First Young Adult Novel Contest

Delacorte Press Contest
Random House, Inc.
1540 Broadway
New York, NY 10036

If you win this contest, you get a $1,500 cash prize, a $6,000 advance against royalties, and your book will be published. The novel should be for readers aged twelve to eighteen. This is a tough contest, because adults can enter it, too, but submissions from young people are welcomed.

Louise Louis/Emily F. Bourne Student Poetry Award

Poetry Society of America
15 Gramercy Park
New York, NY 10003

This contest is open to students in grades nine through twelve. The award goes to the best unpublished poem by a student, and there is a cash prize of $250.

Merlyn's Pen Magazine Contest and Critique

P.O. Box 910

East Greenwich, RI 02818

www.merylnspen.com

Open to students in grades six through twelve, this contest awards $250–$500 as first and second place prizes. Every entry is critiqued by a professional reviewer. The contest is broken down by age group. The winning submissions are published in *Merlyn's Pen*.

National Geographic for Kids

1145 17th Street NW

Washington, DC 20036-4688

www.nationalgeographic.com/ngforkids

This magazine runs different writing contests throughout the year. Check their Web site for updated information.

National Peace Essay Contest

P.O. Box 27720

Central Station

Washington, DC 20038-7720

This essay contest is open to students in grades nine through twelve and is sponsored by the United States Institute of Peace. There is a new essay topic every year, so be sure to get the most current information. The first-place winner in this national competition gets $10,000. Second place gets $5,000, third place gets $3,500. A $1,000 college scholarship is awarded to first-place state winners.

National Written & Illustrated By . . .

Awards Contest for Students

Landmark Editions, Inc.

P.O. Box 270169

1402 Kansas Avenue.

Kansas City, MO 64127

This contest publishes books by students. Write to Landmark Editions for the most up-to-date information.

National Writer's Club

1450 S. Havana, Suite 620

Aurora, CO 80012

The National Writer's Club sponsors annual contests for writers of articles, essays, novels, poems, and short stories. Rules vary for each contest, so write to get an entry form and details.

Time Education Program—Writing & Art Competition for High School Students

P.O. Box 1000

Mount Kisco, NY 10549

Please send a self-addressed, stamped envelope for current rules. Prizes range from $500 to $5,000.

Cool Books
for Cool
Readers

Here's a list of books you may actually enjoy.
You should know that reading is a surefire
way to improve your writing abilities. But
reading stories, novels, and poetry will help
you do much more than improve your writing.
You can read for entertainment and for escape.
You can also find out about the lives of young
people like yourself who have grown up in
places, cultures, or time periods different from
your own. It's just like going on a trip, except
that you don't have to worry about the
driving.

The following list includes books
recommended by teachers, librarians, and—
most importantly—other young people. Check
out the books in your library, and take home
the ones that seem interesting to you. If you
like a book, you can ask your parents, friends,
teacher, or librarian to recommend others like

it. But if you're not hooked after you've read a few chapters of a book, don't worry about it. Try something else. Nobody's grading you!

Adams, Douglas. *The Hitchhiker's Guide to the Galaxy.* (Science Fiction, Humor)

The first book in a series that includes *The Restaurant at the End of the Universe; Life, the Universe, and Everything; So Long, and Thanks For All the Fish;* and *Mostly Harmless.*

Alcott, Louisa May. *Little Women.* (Classic)

Block, Francesca Lia. *Weetzie Bat.* (Contemporary Fiction)

The first book in a series which has also been published in the volume, *Dangerous Angels: The Weetzie Bat Books.*

Blume, Judy. *Tiger Eyes.* (Contemporary Fiction)

Blume has written many other popular books for young people, including *Blubber* and *Just as Long as We're Together.*

Burnett, Frances Hodgson. *The Secret Garden.* (Classic)

Carroll, Lewis. *Alice's Adventures in Wonderland.* (Classic)

Alice's adventures continue in *Through the Looking Glass.*

Creech, Sharon. *Walk Two Moons*. (Contemporary Fiction)

Creech has written other novels for young people, including *Chasing Redbird* and *The Wanderer*.

Cooper, Susan. *The Dark Is Rising*. (Fantasy)

The first book in the series that includes *Greenwitch, The Grey King,* and *Silver on the Tree. Over Sea, Under Stone* is the prequel to this series.

Cormier, Robert. *The Chocolate War*. (Contemporary Fiction)

Dorris, Michael. *The Window*. (Contemporary Fiction)

Dorris also wrote about the main character of this novel, Rayona, in his debut novel, *A Yellow Raft in Blue Water*.

Hinton, S. E. *The Outsiders*. (Contemporary Fiction)

S. E. Hinton wrote this novel when she was a high school junior.

Fitzgerald, John D. *The Great Brain*. (Historical Fiction)

The first book in a series that includes *More Adventures of the Great Brain, Me and My Little Brain, The Great Brain at the Academy, The Great Brain Reforms, The Return of the Great Brain,* and *The Great Brain Does it Again.*

George, Jean Craighead. *Julie of the Wolves*. (Contemporary Fiction)

George has written two other books about Julie, *Julie* and *Julie's Wolf Pack*, as well as *My Side of the Mountain*.

Hughes, Langston. *The Dream Keeper and Other Poems*. (Poetry)

Konigsburg, E. L. *From the Mixed-Up Files of Mrs. Basil E. Frankweiler*. (Contemporary Fiction)

Lee, Gus. *China Boy*. (Contemporary Fiction)
Also read the sequel, *Honor and Duty*.

LeGuin, Ursula. *A Wizard of Earthsea*. (Fantasy)

The first book in a series that includes *The Tombs of Atuan*, *The Farthest Shore*, and *Tehanu*.

L'Engle, Madeleine. *A Wrinkle in Time*. (Science Fiction, Contemporary Fiction)

L'Engle's series about the Murry family continues in *A Swiftly Tilting Planet*, *A Wind in the Door*, and *Many Waters*. Also try *A Ring of Endless Light*, a favorite in her series about Vicky Austin and her family.

Lewis, C. S. *The Lion, the Witch, and the Wardrobe*. (Classic, Fantasy)
The first book written in the *Chronicles of Narnia*.

Montgomery, Lucy Maude. *Anne of Green Gables*. (Classic)
Anne Shirley's story continues in *Anne of Avonlea* and *Anne of the Island*. *Rainbow Valley* and *Rilla of Ingleside* are about her children. Also try Montgomery's series about Emily Starr: *Emily of New Moon, Emily Climbs*, and *Emily's Quest*.

Myers, Walter Dean. *Hoops*. (Contemporary Fiction)
Myers has written dozens of books, including *Fallen Angels* and *Monster*.

Nye, Naomi Shihab. *Habibi*. (Contemporary Fiction)

Paterson, Katherine. *Bridge to Terabithia*. (Contemporary Fiction)
Other popular books by Paterson include *The Great Gilly Hopkins, The Master Puppeteer*, and *Jacob Have I Loved*.

Paulsen, Gary. *Nightjohn*. (Historical Fiction)
Paulsen has also written a sequel, *Sarny*, as well as many adventure books, including *Hatchet*, the first in a series.

Rawls, Wilson. *Where the Red Fern Grows*. (Classic)

Rowling, J. K. *Harry Potter and the Sorcerer's Stone*. (Fantasy)
The first book in a wildly popular series that includes *Harry Potter and the Chamber of Secrets*, *Harry Potter and the Prisoner of Azkaban*, and *Harry Potter and the Goblet of Fire*.

Salinger, J. D. *Catcher in the Rye*. (Classic)

de Saint-Exupery, Antoine. *The Little Prince*. (Classic, Fantasy)

Soto, Gary. *Baseball in April and Other Stories*. (Contemporary Fiction)
Also try Soto's novel *Crazy Weekend*, and *Neighborhood Odes*, a collection of his poetry.

Staples, Suzanne Fisher. *Shabanu: Daughter of the Wind*. (Contemporary Fiction)
Shabanu's story continues in *Haveli*.

Taylor, Mildred D. *Roll of Thunder, Hear My Cry*. (Historical Fiction)

Tolkien, J. R. R. *The Hobbit*. (Fantasy)
The prequel to the *Lord of the Rings* series, which includes *The Fellowship of the Ring*, *The Two Towers*, and *The Return of the King*.

Voigt, Cynthia. *Homecoming*. (Contemporary Fiction)

The first book about Dicey Tillerman's family and friends; others include *Dicey's Song*, *A Solitary Blue*, and *Seventeen Against the Dealer*.

Wojciechowska, Maia. *Shadow of a Bull*. (Fiction)

Yep, Laurence. *Dragonwings*. (Historical Fiction)

Also try Yep's other novels about Chinese-American life, *Child of the Owl* and *Dragon's Gate*.

Zindel, Paul. *The Pigman*. (Contemporary Fiction)

And here are a few books about writing that you may want to check out.

Bird by Bird: Some Instructions on Writing and Life, by Anne Lamott

This book takes a funny, helpful look at the writing process, with a focus on writing fiction.

If You Want to Write: A Book About Art, Independence, and Spirit, by Brenda Ueland

This book is for writers at all levels. It begins with the statement, "Everybody is talented, original, and has something important to say."

Writing Down the Bones: Freeing the Writer Within, by Natalie Goldberg

Goldberg bases her writing practice on Zen philosophy. This book includes encouraging short pieces about writing and suggestions about writing practice that can be used to write everything from poetry to essays and reports.

Answers

✍ **QUIZ #1** ✍

The Parts of Speech

The first **thing** <u>n</u> that struck Manfred's **eyes** <u>n</u> was a group of his **servants** <u>n</u> **endeavoring** <u>v</u> to raise something that appeared to him a mountain of **sable** <u>adj</u> plumes. He **gazed** <u>v</u>, without believing his **sight** <u>n</u>.

"What are **you** <u>pro</u> doing?" cried Manfred, **wrathfully** <u>adv</u>. "Where is **my** <u>pro</u> son?"

A volley of voices replied, "**Oh** <u>int</u>! My lord! The prince! The prince! The **helmet** <u>n</u>! The helmet!"

Shocked <u>v</u> with these **lamentable** <u>adj</u> sounds, and dreading he knew not what, he advanced **hastily** <u>adv</u>; **but** <u>conj</u> what a sight for a father's eyes! **He** <u>pro</u> beheld his child dashed to pieces **and** <u>conj</u> almost buried **under** <u>prep</u> an **enormous** <u>adj</u> helmet, a hundred times more large than any casque ever made for human being, and shaded **with** <u>prep</u> a proportionable **quantity** <u>n</u> of **black** <u>adj</u> feathers.

✍ QUIZ #2 ✍
Coming to Agreements

1. <u>Each</u> of Lorraine's sons (has, have) a frog and several pet otters.

2. Mandy's <u>collection</u> of rubber chickens, clown noses, and brightly colored wigs (were, was) respected throughout the entire circus world.

3. (Is, Are) <u>Kevin and Kyle</u> coming to camp this summer?

4. <u>All</u> of the girls in Smallville (wear, wears) bows in their hair.

5. <u>Mathematics</u> (is, are) my best subject in school.

6. My bride <u>Patricia</u>, my wife and my love, (arrive, arrives) on the steamer from Portugal today.

7. <u>Bees and pollen</u> (irritate, irritates) me the most.

✍ QUIZ #3 ✍
What Kind of Comparison?

<u>M</u> 1. Stefano's eyes were limpid pools of Caribbean water glistening in the sun.

<u>S</u> 2. Watching Uncle Louie dance was like watching Jell-O on springs.

A 3. Love is sometimes like an avocado in winter: You have to pay a high price for it, it can be very hard at first, it tends to rot before it ripens, and you find out too late it was mainly a big pit.

S 4. Larry's feet were like two canoes with leather soles.

M 5. The sun, her cheeks blushed red with embarrassment, hid her face behind the horizon.

✍ QUIZ #4 ✍
The Perils of Punctuation

1. When planning my birthday party, I decided I wanted cake, ice cream, and candy; instead Mom gave us carrots, yogurt, and prunes.

2. There are three essentials for enjoyable road trips: chocolate doughnuts, sunglasses, and a good selection of heavy metal cassette tapes.

3. I'm afraid we're all out of the yellow leather miniskirts; however, I can offer you this polyester parka.

4. I saw a three-toed sloth—considered a delicacy by the natives, who stuff it with pineapple and serve it at feasts—slowly make its way down the diving board, where it paused briefly before doing a swan dive into the pool.

5. We used Christmas lights—both yellow and white—to decorate the gloomy hallway.

6. Get me the hammer—the big heavy one in the black toolbox—so I can squash this bug.

7. "Let's go see the latest Jim Carrey movie, <u>The Drooling Idiot</u>, at the theater tonight!" yelled Mark, but Stacey's stereo was turned up so loud she didn't hear him.

8. Carol was reading one of her mother's books, <u>Poems About Armadillos</u>, when she ran across a poem called "The Pouting Armadillo" that was so sad she was moved to tears.

9. Both of my sisters' hairstyles are so scary they look like they should be starring in <u>The Bride of Frankenstein</u>.

10. "Fido just hasn't been the same since Mr. Johnson's cat took over his doghouse," said Pete.

✍ QUIZ #5 ✍
Looking into Libraries

1. Dewey Decimal System, Library of Congress Classification

2. author cards, title cards, subject cards, cross-reference or "see also" cards

   Bonus Answer: Melvil Dewey

3. (c) Upper left-hand corner

4. newspaper, journal, magazine or three specific titles of newspapers, journals, or magazines

5. on the shelf or on microfilm/microfiche

✍ QUIZ #6 ✍
Too Broad, Too Narrow, or Just Right?

1. B
2. O.K.
3. N
4. O.K.
5. B

6. N
7. N
8. B
9. B
10. O.K.

✍ QUIZ #7 ✍
Outlining Backwards

Your outline might look different from this one. That's okay. The outline below is just a guideline.

I. Introduction

II. The place of cats in ancient Egypt

  A. Cats worshipped and considered sacred

    1. Goddess of warmth of sun, Bubastis, had head of a cat

    2. Cats associated with Bubastis because they like sun

  B. Pampered pets of pharaohs

  C. Killing cats punishable by death

III. The place of cats in ancient Rome

  A. Cats were symbols of liberty and freedom

  B. Goddess of liberty often featured with a cat at her feet

  C. Why? Cats are independent and free-spirited

IV. The place of cats in the Middle Ages

  A. Cats had it hard after fall of Rome

  B. Cats considered "familiars"

    1. Definition: spirit slave of witch or wizard

2. Origin of belief: legend of Galenthias, servant of Hecate

C. Satan and cats

    1. People believed devil disguised himself as a black cat

    2. Superstition about black cats bringing bad luck

D. Cats blamed for Black Death

    1. Plague killed 1/8 to 1/3 of Europe

    2. Cats hunted and killed

    3. Rat-borne fleas later discovered to have caused the plague

V. The Place of Cats Today

A. Pets once again

B. Dog lovers don't like cats (holdover from Middle Ages?)

C. Cat lovers, like ancient Romans, respect cat attitude

VI. Conclusion

Make the Transition

Below are the most likely choices for transitions in the paragraphs. You may have come up with others that work just as well.

1. (A) first
   (B) next, then
   (C) soon, then, finally
   (D) for instance, for example
   (E) after

2. (A) more importantly
   (B) then
   (C) finally
   (D) however, on the other hand

✍ QUIZ #9 ✍
I Got Rhythm!

1. I <u>set</u> her <u>on</u> my <u>pacing steed</u>,
    And <u>nothing else</u> saw <u>all</u> day <u>long</u>,
For <u>side</u>long <u>would</u> she <u>bend</u>, and <u>sing</u>
    A <u>fae</u>ry's song.

2. Be<u>cause</u> I <u>could</u> not <u>stop</u> for <u>Death</u>,
    He <u>kindly stopped</u> for <u>me</u>;
The <u>car</u>riage <u>held</u> but <u>just</u> our<u>selves</u>
And <u>Immortality</u>.

3. For the <u>moon</u> never <u>beams</u> without <u>bringing</u>
    me <u>dreams</u>
        Of the <u>beau</u>tiful <u>Anna</u>bel <u>Lee</u>;
And the <u>stars</u> never <u>rise</u> but I <u>feel</u> the bright
<u>eyes</u>
        Of the <u>beau</u>tiful <u>Anna</u>bel <u>Lee</u>;

4. <u>One</u> if by <u>land</u> and <u>two</u> if by <u>sea</u>
        And <u>I</u> on the <u>opposite shore</u> will <u>be</u>,
<u>Ready</u> to <u>ride</u> and <u>spread</u> the a<u>larm</u>
        Through <u>every</u> <u>Mid</u>dlesex <u>vill</u>age and
<u>farm</u>.

5. "The <u>time</u> has <u>come</u>," the <u>Wal</u>rus <u>said</u>,
        "To <u>talk</u> of <u>many</u> <u>things</u>:
Of <u>shoes</u>—and <u>ships</u>—and <u>sealing-wax</u>—
        Of <u>cab</u>bages—and <u>kings</u>—
And <u>why</u> the <u>sea</u> is <u>boiling</u> <u>hot</u>—
        And <u>whe</u>ther <u>pigs</u> have <u>wings</u>."

Can You Stand the Assonance?

<u>a</u>   1. I met a tr<u>a</u>veler from <u>an</u> <u>an</u>tique l<u>an</u>d
        Who said: Two v<u>a</u>st and trunkless legs
        of stone
        St<u>an</u>d in the desert . . .

<u>o</u>   2. Leave <u>no</u> black plume as a t<u>o</u>ken of
        that lie thy s<u>ou</u>l hath sp<u>o</u>ken!
        Leave my l<u>o</u>neliness unbr<u>o</u>ken!—quit
        the bust above my d<u>oo</u>r!

<u>o</u>   3. He took his v<u>o</u>rpal sw<u>o</u>rd in hand:
        Long time the manx<u>o</u>me f<u>oe</u> he
        sought—

<u>e</u>   4. Let others fr<u>ee</u>ze with angling r<u>ee</u>ds,
        And cut their legs with shells and
        w<u>ee</u>ds.

<u>o</u>   5. I stand amid the r<u>oa</u>r
        Of a surf-t<u>o</u>rmented sh<u>o</u>re.

A Little Alliteration

<u>c</u>   1. <u>C</u>old are the <u>cr</u>abs that <u>cr</u>awl on yonder
        hills,
        <u>C</u>older the <u>c</u>ucumbers that grow
        beneath.

<u>p,c</u> 2. <u>P</u>ale, beyond <u>p</u>orch and <u>p</u>ortal,
        <u>C</u>rowned with <u>c</u>alm leaves she stands

Who gathers all things mortal
    With <u>cold</u> immortal hands.

<u>d</u>   3. <u>Deep</u> into that <u>darkness</u> peering, long I
      stood there wondering,
        fearing,
      <u>Doubting</u>, <u>dreaming</u> <u>dreams</u> no mortal
      ever <u>dared</u> to <u>dream</u> before

<u>f,w</u> 4. The <u>flowers</u> do <u>fade</u>, and <u>wanton</u> <u>fields</u>
      To <u>wayward</u> <u>winter</u> reckoning yields.

<u>f,r</u> 5. Time drives the <u>flocks</u> from <u>field</u> to
      <u>fold</u>,
      When <u>rivers</u> <u>rage</u>, and <u>rocks</u> grow
      cold . . .

About the Author

C. L. Brantley has worked for The Princeton Review since 1991 as an editor and author. Before teaming up with The Princeton Review, she worked in the software, telecommunications, and entertainment industries as a copywriter and speech writer.

She holds a B.A. in English and M.S. in mass communication. She currently resides in Texas, after several long years in New York City. Her favorite color is red, and her favorite saying is, "Hey, at least I'm not dead." She sincerely hopes that you enjoy this book.